PLAY
AND
EDUCATION

PLAY

AND

EDUCATION

THE BASIC TOOL FOR
EARLY CHILDHOOD LEARNING

By

OTTO WEININGER, Ph.D.

Department of Applied Psychology
Ontario Institute for Studies in Education
Toronto, Ontario, Canada

CHARLES C THOMAS • PUBLISHER
Springfield • Illinois • U.S.A.

Published and Distributed Throughout the World by
CHARLES C THOMAS ● PUBLISHER
Bannerstone House
301-327 East Lawrence Avenue, Springfield, Illinois, U.S.A.

© *1979, by* CHARLES C THOMAS ● PUBLISHER
ISBN 0-398-03845-7
Library of Congress Catalog Card Number: 78-14857

With THOMAS BOOKS *careful attention is given to all details of manufacturing and design. It is the Publisher's desire to present books that are satisfactory as to their physical qualities and artistic possibilities and appropriate for their particular use.* THOMAS BOOKS *will be true to those laws of quality that assure a good name and good will.*

Printed in the United States of America
V-R-2

Library of Congress Cataloging in Publication Data

Weininger, Otto, 1929-
  Play and education.

  Bibliography: p. 175
  Includes index.
  1. Play. 2. Education, Preschool. I. Title
LB1137.W44   372.1'3   78-14857
ISBN 0-398-03845-7

FOREWORD

THIS book is about children learning.

The young child, between birth and the age of four or five, plays to his heart's content at home. He finds many different kinds of materials to play with: at first he may play with his developing *sight*: he observes, he watches, he begins to discriminate patterns, shapes, people. He does this in an exploratory way and no one pushes him to do this activity faster or better, no one tells him that he is not seeing things correctly, no one says, "See it my way." We wait for a period of time, during which we tell ourselves that he is a neuropsychologically immature organism and so he may be given the time to explore, to play with his sight. Even when he reaches the level of discriminating between mother and father, we still allow him to play.

We help him to play at different kinds of activities by enriching and changing his environment at times when he is ready for such changes. We add another poster to his wall, we add a trinket to the mobile that is hanging above his bed, or we give him a plastic bottle and clothes pegs of different colors to play with. As he is involved in these activities, he will show changes in his coordination, and he will exercise his responses over and over again. We watch the young child pass his hand over his eyes, we watch him play with his fingers, maybe even suck them, we watch him play with his toes, maybe even pull off his socks, we watch him turn his head, roll on his side, even turn over.

He is encouraged to indulge in this play, because we think that the growth and development of the child is proceeding through a gradual evolution; exercise of his muscles is in actuality a learning process, a learning about himself and what he can do. Growth goes along naturally; however, unless active

v

play behaviour accompanies growth, a general dampening and slowness will start to make its appearance in the child's response to environmental stimuli.

ACKNOWLEDGMENTS

I WOULD like to thank many people for helping me prepare this book, but most of all I want to thank those children with whom I had the opportunity of working; this was a very special time for me and I hope they were able to get as much out of our relationships as I did. They taught me a great deal, not only who I am and how I work, but also how to approach them, when to push and when to hold back, when to change their environment and when to maintain it, even at the expense of someone telling me "why don't you change this dreary room?" Working with teachers has been especially exciting. Finding out why some of our ideas work and why others first need much alteration has been challenging. Perhaps most of us find giving up some pet idea is very hard to do, but I think I have learned that, when working with children and teachers and educators in general, flexibility must be the keynote and understanding must be the thread that runs through all our work.

Ruth Kolenoff remained a loyal friend throughout the rocky course of this book's development and I thank her very much for all her help, criticism, and advice.

Ordinarily I've noticed that authors thank their family for their patience during the writing of a book. I want to thank my family for being there, showing me how people learn and how much children learn at home. We often talked about how school was dull and uninteresting and how much more the teacher would get from my children if she only tried to tap the reservoir of their interests, their explorations, and their "outside school pursuits." Some teachers did, many did not. I have tried to bring together some of my work with education so that other children may feel their teacher's sincere interest and encouragement.

I want to thank the editors of *The Educational Courier; The Journal of Early Childhood Education; Education; Involvement; The Journal of the Canadian Association for Young Children;* and *Orbit,* for publishing some of my work and for allowing me to use parts of the previously published articles in this book.

CONTENTS

PLAY
AND
EDUCATION

SECTION I

A VERY SHORT STORY

Once upon a time, long ago and far away, there were two little children who grew up together. All day long, from sunrise to sunset, they played, asked questions, explored quiet places, jumped over creeks, and collected stones, feathers, rubber bands, and twigs; they talked, laughed, cried, and cuddled; their eyes shone when the wind blew in their faces, or they played with tiny kittens, or they made up stories about giants; the grown-ups who lived with these children debated as to when to start to teach the children, and how, and what, and in what order. This debate waged long and hot over the cold winter months, year after year, until suddenly the children were grown. "Oh dear," said the adults, "we haven't taught them anything important." But the children lived happily ever after, wise in the ways and wonders of the wide world, much to the consternation of the adults, for the adults did not know what the children sensed: Play is a child's way of learning. "Play is the way a child learns what no one can teach him."

The story is ours, the quotation Lawrence Frank's,[16] a well-known educator; the point is the same, too often we try too hard to *give* what children must *gain* for themselves from their experiences of the world.[30,12]

CHAPTER 1

PLAY AND THE YOUNG CHILD

F ROM the time of Plato, philosophers and educators have pointed to the necessity for including play in the educational opportunities provided for young children. Since the *activity* of the child is play, the most natural and efficient way for a child to acquire competency in any curricular area is through play activity. However, if I were to suggest that play, as an educational practice, be extended beyond the kindergarten's four walls, I would risk currying the favour of kindergarten teachers at the expense of provoking the indignation not only of the many teachers of grades one, two, and three but also of the parents of the children in these grades. I would also be suggesting a revolution of sorts. Fortunately, however, what for some people is an unfamiliar way of looking at something does not make it wrong, only discomforting.

Play is not merely a form of activity. It is through play that the young child recreates the world and comes to understand it; his play is predicated on his experiences. Play is not aimless or purposeless or undirected. It is the child's attempt to achieve, to feel comfortable, and hence to be able to innovate and change his world.

I can give you a simple, everyday classroom occurrence. A group of children come running into the classroom — they appear to be poorly controlled. But, while coming in this way, they explore the slipperiness of the floor, the bumping up against other people, and the hurting of themselves on objects as they run and stop. They are learning to see danger and comprehend it in terms of themselves. This is much more effective than telling them that if they do not stop, they will slip and possibly hurt themselves. They are learning from their own actions and those of the other children, because children are generally their own best teachers. By this, I do not mean the teacher can permit dangerous objects to be part of the class-

room or to refrain from intruding upon the childrens' activity
when outside the limits of accepted safety.

The adult takes a disparaging view of the child's world: "Oh,
he isn't doing anything important, he's only playing;" or perhaps the teacher, attempting to hurry the child along on his
daily routine, will say, "Hurry up and finish your reading and
then you can play 'til it's time to go home;" or the weary
parents at the end of a long weekend of noise and questions
and activity will shout, "Stop that playing around and do
something useful." In all three instances, and in thousands
more like them daily, adults are assuming that the child who is
playing is not doing anything "useful," that play is a time-
filler and a way of bribing children to stay out of the way and
keep quiet, or, even more commonly, that play is something
children do to relax between bouts of "learning." In all these
cases the adults are oversimplifying the effects of play for
children and ignoring the influence of play on the development, physically, mentally, and emotionally, of children of all
ages.

Play, far from being as simple as it looks, and as unimportant as it is often judged to be by adults, is in fact the child's
major way of learning, from his earliest infancy.[50]

Just look at the concepts he is exploring! He is involved in
language development as he discusses what to do next with
others and as he makes up stories and simple acting-out situations; he is involved in primitive map-making as he lays out
the village or train station or road; he is seeing for himself
science concepts which he might not be able to deal with verbally for some time, such as the use of the wheel, ramp, pulley,
or lever. He is also learning the elementary physical and math-
ematical concepts about size and shape embodied in "I need
two more blocks," or "I need square blocks now," or "This
building is too tall so it falls down."

The child tests, evaluates, reevaluates, ponders, comprehends,
and works out the actual experiences afforded him by reality.
He uses fantasy in play, and the fantasy becomes reality as he
plays. When the playing cannot conform to adult reality, the
fantasy changes; this can be observed by shifts in the play of the

child. The processes of thinking, of comprehension, of reevaluation, and of perception become important as tools permitting the child to make use of play to correct the fantasy of his experiences. The child is, essentially, formulating a personal schema, a personal cognitive map which enables him to begin to understand the world about him in more or less objective terms. These functions — perception, comprehension, reevaluation, etc. — are the ingredients of his later capacities to use intelligence. Through play the child is formulating the foundation for potential use of intelligence.[44,32]

Through play he begins to acquire some of the first concepts required if he is to grow and develop and then begin to make use of the conceptual skills which we all want him to acquire.

Almost everybody accepts the idea that we put children into classrooms for at least ten years of their early lives so they can learn things they need to know to live in our society. In every learning situation, regardless of the age or grade level of the learner, two aspects of human development are involved — cognitive growth and self or personality development. This is readily acknowledged by learning experts in general, be they educators or psychologists.[5,52] However, there is no denying that a wide gap separates learning experts once they move to a discussion of the specifics of educational practice. Doubtless, more than one factor is responsible for this gap in communication among educators, but one important contributory factor can be presumed to lie in the basic differences between educators as to what an education entails, and in the face of this, what the roles of the teacher and the pupil ought to be.[4,1]

On the one side we find aligned those educators who believe that an education involves, primarily, acquisition of content. For them, the pupil's role becomes that of passive recipient, with the teacher assuming the more active role of content-dispenser, i.e. an adult trained to anticipate the problems the child is likely to encounter and so provide him with a prepared set of rules or concepts to be memorized and applied as ready "answers." For these educators, the intellectual aspect of the child is of primary importance, with self or personality development given lip service. On the other side, we find aligned those educators who believe that education involves, primarily, self or personality development best realized through self-discovery methods of learning. It follows, then, that for these educators the pupil's role becomes that of active participant, with the teacher assuming the less dominant role of observer-guide and learning-environmentalist. Under the tutelage of such a knowledgeable and sensitive adult, it is presumed that each child will come to develop the cognitive skills and self-awareness necessary to the formulation of meaningful concepts, the generation of personal rules, and the development of value judgments.[45, 48] Educators on either side can find support for their particular positions in contemporary psychological learning theories.[37]

It is important for all of us — not only those bound closely to the educational system — to stop now and then and reexamine exactly why we are putting children into classrooms: What do we intend them to learn? How does that learning most fruitfully occur, and where and in what ways are we failing? As you have probably surmised, I intend to focus on the *value* of self-discovery learning — through the child's natural medium of play. By value, I mean the value to the development of the *whole* child — intellectually, emotionally, and bodily.

There are two important ideas to remember when we talk about play and young children which are frequently blurred or misunderstood by adults. The first is that in play, as in all learning, *it is the process, not the product, that is important.* Just as I want the child to understand *how* and *why* 4 × 4 = 16 in order that the answer is not simply a memorized fact, so am I interested in the child playing in his own way, at his own rate, with materials largely of his own choice, to ensure that what emerges is a surer understanding and foundation for the child. I am not really interested in what the play looks like to adult observers, or in any product of it. A child playing with crayons and paper is experimenting, and what the product looks like is unimportant. It is not for us to label it as a house, or a person, or a spaceship, or to compare it with the work of other children and decide it is not "good" enough. I am talking about ways of knowing the how of things, not the what. In any learning task, if the process is not understandable to the child, if he does not follow the necessary sequential steps to reach a goal, then the child may say, "Okay, I'll memorize this," and, in fact, he can do a pretty good job of doing so and will present the product for adult judgment. But what happens in six months, when he goes on to learn something which is based on a true understanding of what he has previously simply memorized? He will be unable to grasp this newer concept because it involves understanding a process which he detoured in order to more quickly reach a product desired by adults. This is a certain way to make learning both limited and unsatisfying for children in the long run.

The second important idea is that we are not talking here about games, but about play. The two are different, although play developmentally leads to games. Games have obstacles and rules imposed by the game itself, whereas play essentially has no rules or obstacles unless these are imposed by the child and hence changeable by the child as well. This question of altering the rules is important, because it allows the child to function for a time in a narcissistic, almost omnipotent, way. The child needs to find out how well he can do things for himself, to change rules and still master the situation. A feeling of mastery over reality is extremely important for the child, particularly between the ages of three and six. His picture of *himself* is acquired by achieving mastery *by himself* over the obstacles he *sets himself*, not by having adults tell him he is nice or good at something. Unless adults interfere by setting unrealistic standards, such as being able to draw a "real" house like an older sibling, most children will very realistically set goals they can reach and make up rules which fit their skills and abilities. This is a natural and sensible way to develop a feeling of self-worth and not one which adults should interfere with by changing the child's play into games before the child is ready for this kind of transition.

This leads to one of the most important goals for the young child, an exceptionally important aspect in the child's development as a personality: *identification.* A young child has to be able to identify with an adult human being, to relinquish part of his omnipotence for that which he sees in adults. This is necessary if he is to begin to view himself as someone who does not have all the information, but who needs to begin to rely on the adult to gain this information. If the child thinks that there is nothing for him to learn, because he knows it all, then accepting information from adults is either absent or at a very low level. The omnipotent child thinks there is no reason to regard what the adult says as important, for "I know it all." Only after the child has seen the need to identify with the more powerful adult, the adult who can alter "things" and who can provide for safety and freedom, does the child gradually give up part of his own omnipotence for that of the adult. He begins to look towards the adult as a provider, as a strong person, as a safety person, and as a fund of information. His identification with such a person is necessary if he is going to be able to accept what the adult has to say. Before this can happen, the child must have some understanding of himself; self-respect, self-mastery, self-confidence, a sense of self-worth and of self-affirmation, of I AM. These qualities are in large measure achieved through playing, naturally and in his own time and his own way, without needless adult pressures to "measure up," or "be the same as," or "do it the right (adult) way." After the child has achieved this form of identification with adults and a strong sense of self, then, and only then, will he really be ready to play games with imposed rules without having it make him feel less competent, less satisfactory, At this stage, games permit the development of social attitudes and encourage the child to learn to be with others, to cope with and fit into a structure; in other words, games are part of the process of socialization. They give adults a chance to evaluate the child's capacity to accept rules, to work with others, to have a specific aim to work towards, and form social relationships.

Play, then, is an integral part of the child's being, it is the business of childhood, and it has a unique and vital role in the *whole* educational process. It is through his play that he grows, and the growth in turn acts as a stimulus to play-change, which is learning. The relationship is a reciprocal, totally integrated one: play and growing — growing and play.[33]

I believe it is essential that early childhood education provide flexible and adaptable ways of giving instruction. The child must be provided with the opportunity to develop the *ways* to do things, ways he is able to achieve, and ways he is able to gain satisfactions. It is then the role of the teacher to create the classroom atmosphere which will encourage learning and exploration. It is not suggested that the teacher take a laissez-faire attitude, a "wait and see attitude," but rather that the teacher recognize the needs of the children and provide the play and play materials which will encourage them to move on to the next level of learning. It is not suggested that the child just be thrown into a big arena and told to play and learn. Rather, the classroom is an active learning centre which is continuously being assessed and evaluated by the teacher as to its suitability to learning by all the children. The teacher encourages and brings in new materials as she recognizes the need to introduce and/or change the classroom. The potential learning in the classroom is then an interaction process between the play-learning of the children and the catalyst-atmosphere created by the teacher. If the teacher does not recognize the need to change and add new materials, then the learning and play of the children will deteriorate and regress. Problems of behaviour and/or learning are then bound to occur. It is necessary for the teacher to continually assess, to watch and listen to the children, and to act as the catalyst for the play and learning of the children. The teacher is the resource person; the teacher becomes the one with whom the children identify and therefore from whom they accept information and change.

It is the child's feeling of being able to accomplish and achieve that is so vital. I see the need to encourage and promote this feeling in the schools. This is not done by compelling young children to learn, by rote, materials labelled "school learning" but is done by creating the classroom atmosphere for learning through the medium of childhood play. Look carefully at this quote from Pearl S. Buck's *The Joy of Children*:[10]

> For adults the most satisfying hours of life are those spent in interesting and absorbing, exciting work. What such work

provides for adults is provided for children in interesting, absorbing and exciting play. . . . In play, the child finds satisfaction for his entire being, his body is strengthened, his mind refreshed and energized, his imagination inspired.

Play is the work of the child, neither as simple nor as pointless as most adults seem to believe. It is through play that the child gains the satisfactions he needs to allow him to continue to learn other kinds of things we too frequently, and mistakenly, believe are the sole subject matter suitable in schools.

Unfortunately, it is the rule rather than the exception that (throughout Canada and elsewhere) successful completion of kindergarten means, for a child, trading the spaciousness of the kindergarten classroom — with its wealth of interesting toys, props, and varied stimuli calculated to arouse his natural curiosity for a grade one classroom — with desks which curtail freedom of movement and successfully eliminate large working areas. The kindergarten's wide variety of inviting stimuli are missing and so is the spontaneity and openness necessary for the realization of each child's potential through the natural medium of play.

Perhaps behind the adults' reliance on the "playless" system is a major concern that their child will not be able to get a job, or make a living, or fulfill parental professional expectations, or be a success unless he is equipped by the traditional didactic pedagogy. Parents' pleasure with the "facts" the child brings home from his early years at school, his ability to tell colours or count or recite the alphabet, his paying attention to the teacher and being a good boy and doing "homework," and their encouragement of these activities, suggest that specific content reduces their anxieties regarding the child's future. They do not as yet realize that his future is limited by the premature presentation of concepts typical of the traditional educational system. Aside from all the factors already mentioned — curiosity, identity, self-growth — we must keep in mind that the world changes very quickly; a child narrowly educated in some practical or professional role today may be seriously handicapped twenty years from now when much more knowledge, many more fields, will be available.

When I ask "How is a Rabbit?" (see page 173), I truly do not mean "What is a Rabbit?." Education has been too much involved in the "what" of things. Instead it should try to provide the child with opportunities to experience the "howness" of a rabbit: how does it move, how does it wiggle its tail, or eat, or shake its legs, or twitch its nose? Unless the child has developed ways of knowing and learning about things, he may be hopelessly left behind with his old knowledge. The child taught to memorize in 1957 that there are ninety-eight elements, who then had to "unlearn" that "fact" in 1960, and again in 1965, would have been much better off learning how to find out things for himself in the first place.[44]

For all we know our children may be living on the moon: A curious mind and the ability to feel free to explore will stand them in much better stead than the knowledge that there are many continents on earth. It is important, therefore, that educators not allow themselves to be forced into the traditional role of "teacher," a doler-out of facts, control and content oriented, by the anxieties of the current adult system. We must try to evolve a workable educational model with the needs of the children as our first guideline.

CHAPTER 2

THE GROWING SELF

WHEN the infant is exploring his toes, his fingers, and his tongue, he is exploring the "howness" of himself. When he reaches for the mobile hanging above his crib he is interested in what it is and how it is.[53]

A child needs to express himself; develop a sense of security, initiative, social consciousness, and responsibility; and experience the joy of living. This is not a simple, direct, easy growth process; rather, it is complex and paradoxical, requiring a fine balance between moving forward and returning to a previous position for a time, asserting and questioning.

A child finds the business of play intensely absorbing, as all of us who have watched a three- or four-year-old playing have no doubt observed. But he is not "just playing," it is not something for which we merely set aside "fifteen minutes in the large room with the wheeled toys." Play takes place literally every minute of the child's waking life in these early years, and he works as hard at it as any of us do at learning or teaching or working. His ability to play, to have fun, to enjoy himself establishes a very important life pattern, one that says it is okay to enjoy yourself, one that says happiness and security, and fun can be created from within and they are not given to you by someone else. A television set, a new toy, a structured program created by adults, an outing, a plan, these do not guarantee happiness or involvement. Reliance on one's ability to create, to play freely, to enjoy are much more certain sources of happiness than are external sources. In a society in which an increasing amount of leisure time seems to be evolving, keeping this early sense of enjoyment through self-discovery and play is more important than ever.

A baby plays with his toes, his fingers, and anything else he can grasp. Slightly older infants play at hiding and appearing and "finding" — discovery! For a long time play is parallel —

two fifteen-month-olds may be in the same room with the same batch of toys, but their interaction is likely to involve only taking toys from each other and screaming at being dispossessed of something they have "mine!" feelings about.[31] As they grow older and physically surer of themselves, they climb, roll, jump, run, clamber, and rush at everything and everyone, delighted to observe their own growing strength, repeating each action and finding how predictably they can achieve, gaining strength and power over a largely unpredictable world. Later they imitate everything the adult or older child does and play at being grown-ups. Through this play, and then the desire to tell what is happening to themselves, to tell about experiences and the effects they are having on their environment and the effect the environment is having on them, they begin to develop speech patterns and communication skills. Every day the growing, playing child runs into more concepts and ideas about space, movement, texture, weight, size relationships, and people than we could possibly teach, if we had to start from scratch. In fact, educators have not been able to find methods to teach elementary school children effectively the concepts they absorb in their preschool play.

When I outline the development of the growing self I think in terms of the origination and gradual acquisition of a *cognitive map*,[42] or the knowledge that an individual has of life space; that is, an individual, as he progresses through life, constructs an overview of spatial relationships comprising a special space. This is not a simple memory process like turning left or right or declaring "there is a chair here and a table there," but rather an individual is able to construct in his own thinking a comprehensive map of an area. While this cognitive or comprehensive map will give him a general picture of his environment, he will also construct strip maps, which are detailed mappings of specific regions within the larger, comprehensive map. Thus the child is fully aware that the dining room in his house contains a dining table, six chairs and a buffet, with a lamp overhead, a rug on the floor, and a window with curtains. His strip map of this area may contain the details of the rug pattern under the table, which he has used as a road route for his toy automobiles. He has a detailed spatial understanding of the space under the table which is very meaningful for him and becomes organized and understood because of his play. While he is busy with his strip map, the comprehensive map allows him to move about the larger space of the dining room without having to think about avoiding pieces of furniture.

Although I have used the image of spatial relationships here, I do not mean to suggest that the cognitive map is restricted solely to knowledge of physical things or space. As the early years of the growing child are concerned with the physical and emotional, so is the child's developing "map." Both branch out later into the transformation of physical into conceptual, into intellectualization and abstractions, all in the child's good time if the adults don't step in to "adjust" the growing self into their concepts of readiness.

Thus, at times in the child's life the comprehensive map will not only contain the real objects in the space but will be elaborated by imagination and fantasy when there are aspects and details missing and required by him in order to achieve a kind of satisfaction with his environment. He may appear to "distort reality" and make mistakes in an environment he is familiar with, but, in fact, for him it is not a mistake. This distortion is a needed effort to try and enlarge the potential in his world.

It is as though the child, in elaborating the map, has added details or schemes which exist only for him, and in doing so may actually come up with a novel way of coping with his particular environment. If we step in too quickly and try to alter what seems to us to be distortions, then do we not limit creativity? It seems to me that the premature attempted structuring by the adult of this cognitive map limits the child's understanding of his environment.

The sense of self and self-concept begins long before the child enters kindergarten. The child does not start to play when he is about two years old and can move about. The child plays much before this, starting as early as birth. When the child is born he shows certain kinds of integrated activity — sucking, breathing, reflexive action — but his neurological apparatus is not efficient enough at this point to cope with much of his world. The first aspects of this integration which we see are such things as pleasure in the satisfaction of being given sufficient food, pleasure in being warm and contented, pleasure in soft sounds, particularly the cooing sounds of the infant's mother. These pleasurable processes appear to permit an equilibrium to develop between the child and his environment. This equilibrium seems to be the necessary condition to allow for an orderly cognitive functioning learning process which aids the growth of basic neurological processes and psychological characteristics. It follows that the infant denied this basic care and mothering does not evolve and develop effectively.[25]

Not only does the infant seem to spend time trying to achieve this equilibrium, but when it is achieved, the infant then involves himself in seemingly passive looking and listening. He is, in fact, playing with his developing sight and his ability to catch sounds. We've all seen babies lying still and staring at the mother's face, an object, or seeming to listen to a soft sound. This is not accidental but is really a beginning step in formulating a cognitive map of his world, primarily, at this point, the mother's face and her method of feeding. It permits the infant to connect and interrelate such things as mother's voice and food, mother's voice and a teddy bear, mother's touch and mother's smile. It brings activities and experiences together for the child. Essentially, pleasure and the subsequent equilibrium permit passive staring and listening, which in turn act as the urge towards activity on the part of the infant, which is to select stimuli and respond to them. He observes, he watches, he begins to discriminate patterns, shapes, people. He is exploring.[46]

As the baby grows older, he explores greater and greater amounts of his environment, sometimes looking at things in great detail, at other times looking about in a kind of total scan. Now he needs an interesting environment apart from his mother . . . he needs colours, soft, safe toys, mobiles, another poster added to his wall. He passes his hands over his eyes, plays with his fingers and sucks them. We watch with pleasure and pride as he plays with his toes, even pulls off his socks, turns his head, rolls on his side and turns over. We encourage and indulge him in his play, knowing he is learning.

As his explorations continue, essentially expressed as play, satisfaction occurs and his experiences are intrinsically rewarding. The infant does not need external reward — but he does need an environment which encourages play.

As the child becomes a moving person, creeping and crawling, his cognitive maps are extended and include not only the physical aspects of his environment but the tactile, auditory, and kinesthetic details as well. Sounds of activities become more meaningful, and now he can predict what is going on, where it is going on, and how long he might have to wait alone.[54] This is an important and urgent experience for the infant and young child to undergo, for it permits him to evolve an ego function of delay in gratification, to withstand frustration, and to recognize that mother will be here soon to satisfy the needs. It helps the child to hold onto himself, to contain himself, and not "fall apart." This child of six to eight months relates and organizes auditory, physical, and kinesthetic stimuli. He is in the process of testing and putting all things into his mouth and in this way exploring his world, not just on the oral level, but by integrating oral activity with various other stimuli. It is at this point in his life that he is learning a special cognitive style of his own: his way of thinking, acting, playing, to learn about his world. He is responding to his own internal structure, that is, his thinking processes and the feeling states which he receives to various things which are happening to him in his environment. His cognitive style is expressed by his comprehensive map, and the strategies, the self-picture, his interactions with other people are all part of this map which in turn acts as a growing edge to further development.

The curiosity of the young child of twelve months can be expressed because he has the foundation and the security to explore. It is an intrinsic curiosity because he can look upon other aspects of his environment and not suffer from the anxiety of strangeness. Small objects, things which belong to mother, stimulate curiosity because they are things to be looked at. He organizes these small bits into a meaningful whole for himself, and in this way he learns. He is also, of course, learning how to handle his body. He is learning how to move his arms and legs and to gain control over them. He is forming a body image and gaining control over motor skills. Motor function, sensory function, ego development, cognitive development, and a developing balance between these functions occur about the same time. It is essential that the child be looked upon as a functioning whole, with several areas but integrated and competent. We may look at these aspects of his development as though they are separate, but it is urgent to think of them as integrated and functioning in reciprocal fashion. This kind of reciprocity allows the child to go ahead in one specific skill, while holding other skills in abeyance. Thus when he walks, it seems as though he does not chatter as much, but once walking is mastered talking comes back to its original, if not higher, level.[46]

The child who has not been penned up but has been free to play and explore an increasingly large area of the room gains mobility and independence at his own rate. He can play at hiding and appearing, learning a most important thing; that people disappear and reappear. He plays at seeking a "lost" object.[54]

We can see, then, that play has performed many valuable functions for the child from earliest infancy, in a purely sensory-motor way through to the most abstract level, as in word and language play. It has extended the exploratory drive, increasing the sensory input and cognitive awareness of the environment, and provided a major achieving pattern, all of which are closely interwoven with providing for creative growth and development. This creativity, which is one of the most important by-products of play, in turn allows the child to develop a cognitive framework and a network of conceptual development which together comprise learning in its most important sense.

Thus what looks like mere child's play to the unobservant observer is not really that simple at all, but the incredible ability of the human animal to develop himself in almost every waking moment. To play, to explore, to imitate, to manipulate, to experiment is not only in the finite, to learn, but in the infinite, to be.[32]

This creative being actually looks for, in a curious way, things in his environment which will satisfy his curiosity. Young children will try to make use of objects in a new and different way after the first novelty has worn off; that is, after the first attempt to find out something about its reality, the child will go on to make use of it in another way. The plastic bottle, for example, may be at first sucked, then held, then rolled, then banged, then used as a container, then dumped, then used as a building block, and so forth. Curiosity is, it seems, an intrinsic characteristic in the young child. His curiosity and improvements in all areas of competencies are used to create for himself strategies to avoid boredom. This curiosity and the explorative nature the child now exhibits leads him to explore the whole house. He learns and wants to practise what he has learned. The child practises words by repeating them, practises fine motor skills by repeating simple or integrated activities, and he really works hard at trying to master skills. Sometimes he is hurt doing this — he falls, bumps his head, scratches himself. From this he learns further, that pain can be avoided by increasing or improving his dexterity. He learns how to integrate pain in his cognitive field and develops strategies to avoid pain. Pain can be helpful in that it becomes another aspect of his comprehensive map of his world and acts in such a way as to push him to develop new, different, creative strategies to cope with his world.

For this young toddler, then, play is his "work" and helps him understand what is happening around him, inside and outside of himself. He has developed what we could call an "observing ego," a part of himself which allows him to reflect upon and receive information. He is beginning to distinguish the "not me" and to recognize, sometimes with difficulty and pain, what is certainly outside his omnipotent and narcissistic control. His most consistent relationship is still with his mother in most cases. As he plays, he examines his relationship to his mother by testing out, relating to, finding out what is under his control and what is not. There is (as described by D. Winnicott),[54] a *potential space* developed between mother and child, and it is within this space that the child examines his own relationship to his environment, flexing the observing ego. This potential space seems to provide a very safe space within which the child may test out newly learned activities while still being within sight of the mother; later on, having felt the safety of this space, being able to contain it within his mind, he may explore activity outside of this space. Potential space acts almost as fertilizer on earth, for while fertilizer helps seeds to grow, so does the potential space act to provide safety for activities to grow. Fertilizer seems no longer necessary after a period of time, so potential space is no longer necessary. The plant grows, being able to obtain its own nutrients further and further away from itself; so, too, the child grows. The child is able to look further and further afield and gain satisfaction and achievement without having to turn around to see whether mother is watching. However, most unlike the plant, the child wants to come back to mother to relate experiences to her, to tell her what has been going on in his world, to share the event.

In this way, the ego and its perception of reality may become broadened and strengthened and stabilized — providing the child has a playing relationship, a potential space, between himself and his mother. Without this space, I suggest the child will not be able to make use of the concept of the observing ego; that is, the growth of his self would become too closely identified with his mother, her problems and difficulties, and would prevent him from becoming a separate person. It is the potential space, and ensuing confidence, between mother and child which allows him to play, helps the observing ego, and acts as a kind of self-healing mechanism. The child is able to play out and observe some of his own poorly organized, if not inadequate, responses to its environment, in particular to his mother. His play will sometimes lead him to a precipice, where he can explore aspects of his own unconsciousness. The play, because of the precipice, may be frightening to the child and this is when the "space" between him and his mother is most beneficial, for she is not of him but with him; she is not there to stop him from being frightened, but is a solid experience entity to help him work through his fear.

In creating an atmosphere of confidence, the child's self-confidence can develop. There is a feeling of being safe to explore new areas and new ways of working with new people.

As the child grows older — three to four years — he begins to become involved with his community; that is, the self develops in relation to people other than his mother: adult and child neighbours. The child will actively express a desire to do things by himself. This expression is often unrealistic in terms of the demands facing him. However, such demands indicate a growing awareness of the child as a doer, an awareness of some of his own limitations within which he then makes use of the guiding resource person. The child has recognition of his competencies in dealing with the physical world; and in fact this is his major recognition: how he alters the world physically by running, walking, jumping, shouting, and playing.

Another area of the growing self concerns the information he gets in playing with other children. He is beginning to see that he can play with some, but others will not play with him. He learns that there are some places he can play and others where he cannot. He has begun to understand language well enough to comprehend instructions, particularly relating to activities that are of concern to him. He talks about himself. The use of language concerns action and capacities. The values he begins to place are in terms of comparison with relationship to other children as well as adults. "I can; You can't; I have; You haven't; You're stupid; I am not; You're good; I'm bad; etc." The language that he uses now may also be unrealistic, and fantasy plays an important role in his development. Along with language acquisition and development, increased involvement with other people and the inevitable obstacles occur. A sense of self is imperative if he is to cope with the reality of being thwarted as he encounters conflicts between his desires and the rights of other people. Through language, activity, and guidance from the adults in his world, he begins to recognize internal and external standards, of limits of behaviour vis-à-vis other people. The imperious *I* begins to give way to *we* and social relationships evolve. At this time empathy may show, as long as it is not in excess conflict with his desires. This ability to take on another person's point of view is difficult, and to ask for cooperative play before he is ready is to retard the child's capacities to make accurate judgments. The child is essentially an egocentric person: Because he knows something, it must be true and correct. It is difficult for him to accept information from other people. Through play and interaction with his peers, the child gradually changes the egocentric position to one where he is more able to incorporate the ideas, comprehensions, and information of other people; this allows him to accommodate, assimilate, and develop them.

One of the most important aspects now in evidence is the identification the child makes with the adult — mother, father or, later, teacher.[14] In a sense, this identification is a long process whereby the child gradually assumes the role as he understands it, and the internalized feelings that go with the role. This structure is provided for by the parents in their daily caring for the child, and in the child's accepting the care and love given by the parents. In learning by identification, the child has taken on for himself the role which he perceives as being occupied by the father or the mother or the teacher, so when the mother is kind and tender to the new baby, one can often hear, in a quiet voice, the little girl talking to her doll in almost the same way. From adults he observes and absorbs their capacity to cope with frustrations, accept substitutes, delay gratification, shift interests, and generally adapt to the flow of life around them. The ability to deal with difficult situations without getting upset, stopping the learning, or removing oneself from the situation can only be learned through identification, which permits the child to play out the "learning to adapt and getting used to difficult or new situations."

This growing self of three or four years is indicating a growing competency with the physical world. He is block-building, working with toys and materials, developing his fine motor responses. He is playing in the street milieu of his peers and expanding his gross motor needs. His creativity is explored in the production of new approaches, perceptions, and competencies and is seen daily in various specific and concrete things he makes. He is also using language in a definitive way, he is dealing with the social world in terms of now being able to ask for things, being able to interact verbally, communicating, and having needs satisfied.

A child of this age may or may not be in nursery school. Regardless, he is relentlessly moving toward his school years and will become involved in and be the target of the school system with its accompanying priorities of achievements and categorizing of intelligence. Here the child will encounter a different kind of play, in that structure and rules will make their appearance, and this will affect his development.

The rudiments of the child's personality have been formed; the basic life skills are there. One area of his growing self-concept concerns his knowledge of the capacities as practised in routine areas; use of toilet, faucets, dressing, eating, general mobility, stair-climbing, carrying things, and so on. Another sense of the growing self is seen in imitation and the copying of ideas, attitudes, walk, speech, and play with toys of those who surround him; at first, adults and parents and teachers, and increasingly (particularly once he has reached the classroom stage) his peers. The experiences a child has by extension of his classroom help him to observe, to form new relationships, to draw conclusions, to make tentative decisions. These experiences help him to organize perceptions and nourish abilities to look for experiences and, later in life, vocations which will be more fulfilling. First-hand experience is a vital aspect of the child's learning, and the organization of these first-hand experiences through either classroom arrangement into centres and/or extensions into the outside environment are vital for learning.

He will be exposed to input, much of which will be stored in his head. As he plays and reconstructs and creates, he formulates for himself a functioning which is not necessarily communicated linguistically but which seems to be stored in his head and available to him at other times. Because we do not ask him the right questions, we may not realize it is there. However, the child will express the stored information as needed. This information storage and retrieval is a cognitive function.

The retrieval of this knowledge will often be used in ingenious, novel, and creative ways.

The child's early school year, whether nursery school or kindergarten, leads him to express himself — his values, perceptions, insights — in symbolic terms. The early years, under four, are what Lowenfeld[29] described as the *scribble stage*, which is self-explanatory. A child's scribbles should be taken seriously, as they mark his first attempt at self-expression with graphic materials, and no attempt should be made to hurry the scribbler on to more "advanced" stages.

Toward the end of the scribble stage, human figures will appear and be named. These rudimentary symbols are heads with arms attached. When bodies and legs appear, the child has moved to the *preschematic stage*, usually observed in children at age four to seven. It is during this stage that the child begins to discover the relationship that exists between thinking, drawing, and the world of objects and events. During this stage, his symbols are constantly in flux, ever being altered to accord with his new perceptions of reality. Each child develops his own symbols for animals, trees, flowers, buildings, automobiles, etc. At this stage of development, inanimate objects often become endowed with human feelings and expressions, e.g. smiling suns, animals, and houses. Any relationship between the symbols he has painted or drawn on one sheet of paper is purely emotional. Although form is important to him, colour and proportion are subservient to feeling.[23]

The child is now on the threshold of society's institutions, of the place where he will receive his formal training as a member of society. He has indeed developed and grown — created a self — since he first drew breath. The magnitude of his growth is evident when you think of the newborn infant. It has all been achieved through play.

CHAPTER 3

PLAY AND EDUCATION

PLAY is the child's private reality, which we can only briefly glimpse and guess at for any individual child. Since the child's oral ability lags behind his ability to play things out, and since his symbols are not likely to be those which we might ordinarily use, in the final analysis only children know how meaningful their play is for them. Those who have worked or been involved with acutely disturbed children will recognize that it is often the child who seems most unable to play, who simply stands or sits, motionless, nonverbal, who is the most frightening to watch, the one for whom you can hope the least, about whom you worry the most, because he is the one to whom there seems to be no avenue of approach. Some adults will analyze and conceptualize children's play and most adults will continue to accept it as "just kids fooling around," but it is in essence untouchable, a private experience, *a unique and novel and fascinating part of childhood without which it may be impossible to reach adulthood.* A child must play as certainly as he must eat, breathe, and be sheltered and loved, if he is ever to be a whole person in this fragmented world.[6]

Play is the natural avocation of childhood: As children cannot be forced to play, neither do they need to be taught to do so. Play is intrinsically motivated and intrinsically reinforced, a self-generating and extremely satisfying mode of behaviour for the young human being. It follows, then, that play must serve some very important functions for human development, since it is both as natural and as necessary to the young child as the bodily and emotional needs which sustain life itself.

Play does a lot of things for children. First, it's fun — and that is important. If you watch young children play, though, you soon recognize that it is also serious business for them.

26

Play provides the child with experiences and chances to react to the world and to see how the world reacts to him, to learn about the world by playing with it. He experiences air, water, sand, wind, rain, snow, mud, sounds, voices, smells. He learns which things can safely be handled, which cannot; which things disappear, change, or stay the same; he finds out which things he can affect by his own efforts or by his mere presence and which are forces beyond his control or the control of adults. It is hard for most of us to remember, much less recapture, the sense of wonder with which the very young child explores his ever-widening universe and seeks to make of it a predictable, understood pattern. It is an enormous task to categorize all the objects, animate and inanimate, which fill the world in terms of purpose, safety, and origin. The one-year-old child who eats the first rose of his first spring after carefully and solemnly taking off all the petals, one by one, to examine, sniff, feel, and lick them, is playing — and learning.

Play facilitates the cognitive growth of the child by permitting him and encouraging him to *do* rather than being done to or being told what to do. Play is a learning process consisting of sequences involved in creative patterns like changing, designing, questioning, organizing, integrating, simplifying. Play involves judgmental patterns for the child, like understanding, penalizing, combining, comparing, criticizing, evaluating, explaining, and many others. Play involves discriminative patterns such as defining, collecting, contrasting, choosing, describing, communicating, identifying, listening, ordering, matching, classifying, and many others. As the child goes through these patterns in play, he learns to be attentive and to listen, to understand and to perceive, to interpret and then to communicate; and along with this he also remembers what he has done because, for him, this behaviour has been meaningful. It has not been a superimposed aspect of learning but rather has taken into account his particular developmental style and position.

Play helps children to find ways of dealing with their complex and often ambivalent emotional reactions to themselves, to their peers, and to the adults in their world. Play helps them to sort out these feelings, to master what has been frightening or traumatic or exciting. This is accomplished by playing out the event again and again, until it no longer holds any elements which upset or inhibit the child. The child who plays hospital is playing out feelings of fear, anxiety, and anger. The child is afraid to go to the hospital because he does not know what will happen, he is also angry because he has a sense of being ignored by the adults in his world. He expresses all these in his play. Play allows the child to experiment with unresolved situations and to solve the myriad of problems which exist during the exploration of a specific unresolved situation. It allows him to solve these problems for himself. Adults can talk about the things which bother them, until gradually they come to accept or at least to understand them, and to be at peace with themselves. A child lacks the verbal facility of an adolescent or adult; he can cry, become hysterical, be angry or withdraw, but none of these gives him the release adults find in doing any or all of these things coupled with talking it out. The only medium for full expression of his feelings is play, with or without words, until he masters, inasmuch as it is possible, his feelings about the situation which is upsetting him. Until he has had this chance, he is usually unable to proceed to any other situation comfortably and is unable to learn or absorb from such situations because he is blocked and unable to concentrate on the present. This is not too difficult to understand: any adult who has tried to think about something, listen to someone, or perform anything but a rote task when his mind is preoccupied and his feelings engaged in a previous and unresolved dilemma will recognize this reality.

Another function of play is that it serves to integrate behaviour patterns and coordinate experiences. The child playing randomly on the street or in his yard picks up corks, bottles, pieces of junk, leaves, or anything at hand and plays with these in the many ways which catch his fancy, repeating some acts, adding new materials, discarding things he does not find useful or interesting enough any longer. Later he may play with a new object in the same way he played with the rock on the street: a ball in his playroom may be heaved at the wall to see if it will fall back and lie still, or dropped in the toilet to see if it will sink as the rock did in a puddle. Gradually the child builds patterns of what can be expected to happen and when, and coordinates his experiments with things in what is obviously a learning way. Even the baby does this, as he tries everything in his mouth first to see if it is edible; older children try to discover which things can safely be climbed on or pushed over or rolled or thrown, both in terms of their physical properties and of adult reactions to the activity.

Play permits direct learning. It permits the child to explore the thoughts, ideas, and understanding that he has of his inner and outer world and allows him to build his inner world a little closer to reality. Play permits this reaccommodation and correction.

Play is the cognitive map-maker. A child looks at his environment and selects a piece of it to attend to at a particular moment — his activity becomes attentional, he concentrates on the stimuli in the piece of his world which he has selected. As he acquires information from these stimuli, he forms a kind of map in his mind. He has a general overview of what is going on and then he can move on to another piece of his world. As he gets older, the map he is making will become more detailed and different kinds of information will fill it out: it will be more complex, more textured, wider in scope, and the inaccuracies will be replaced with more accurate or complete information. For the young child, information which does not fit into the map in his head will be quickly forgotten or rendered meaningless. If it cannot be assimilated and integrated into what is important or useful to him, it is not likely to be retained. Sometimes it seems as though a child will put a bit of information aside temporarily, sensing it to be of interest but not sure where to put it until he gets to that part of his map where it is relevant; and then a tiny detail or fact which the adult has quite forgotten will surface in his play or talk and become a part of his world view. This kind of cognitive comprehension and organization is obviously an integral part of every learning experience for all human beings: simple studies of things such as digit memory span show that people can memorize many more numbers than can be retained as random bits of information, *if* they make up a pattern which is significant to the individual. Most people spend their whole lives trying to make the world make sense for them. Is it any wonder, then, that children seek constantly to do this through the one medium they can control and manipulate and use as they like, with total flexibility and mastery: that of self-structured play?

Play seems to be a very valuable experience in language development. During play, the child uses speech to verbalize what he is doing. The play and the activity of play act as stimuli to verbalizations; the child's activity and actual experience with objects help him to talk freely and communicate with those who are playing about him. Susan Isaacs[22] has written a very astute insight into the nature of language: ". . . . words are only tokens of experience and are either empty or confusing to the children until they have had enough immediate experience to give the words content. With young children, words are valueless unless they are backed by the true coin of things and doings. They have their own place as aids to experience and to clear thought about experience."

In the classroom the child continues to manipulate, act, and make order out of his world. In doing this, he uses language as a tool to describe what he is doing. He acts upon his environment by movement, by building, by creating and then is able to test this by the stability of the structure which he has created. Once he has found a stability in the structure, he can go on to communicate this stability verbally. It is almost as though play creates the opportunity for preverbal logical thinking and working out of understandings, which then allows him to verbalize his reasoning and logic. He is further aided by the sensitive listening to and questioning by the teacher. Play is the stage that permits the initial activity to unfold, and carries along with it the seemingly separate, but not actually separate, functions of language and reasoning. Through language the child is able to communicate his ideas and to find out the sense of logic and reasoning that is available to him.

What I am stating here is that activity, manipulation, and exploration, all aspects of play, must be the means by which the child builds up his conceptualizations. Skills and competencies cannot be considered as belonging to one subject matter area, to one subject description, but rather flow from one area to another. Reading is not learned by just looking at books, it requires visual-motor play, body-image understanding, black-white sequencing, straight-line conceptualizing, and so on. To learn to read in a vacuum without play is like trying to walk around without legs. The child must be given the opportunity to explore the fullness of his life space, to make many of his own connections, to find out what he can do with his materials and what they can do for him. He is setting up a map of his world and taking pieces of it to explain and to play with his chosen materials. In the same way, subject matter does not really belong in isolated categories, particularly in early childhood, but rather some of the information from one area helps the child understand the information from another area.

At play, children are constantly moving, touching, listening, and looking. Therefore, at play they practise and learn physical skills and sensory discrimination. At play, they are constantly talking and so practise their vocabulary and concepts. At play, they explore and question, increasing their knowledge, skills, and vocabulary. At the same time they practise ways to relate to people, learning the complicated business of human relations. Through imaginative and dramatic play, children make models of the real world and play out situations in order to understand and gain mastery over what they know about the world. By acting out what they have seen people do, they learn to comprehend and understand male and female roles. Play also allows them to act out their fantasies, fears, needs, and wants. Play has the power of relieving the child of anxiety and turmoil, and allows him to absorb information which otherwise would have been threatening or dangerous to him. Thus, play, a learning activity, also makes a great contribution towards personality development, mental health, and emotional well-being.

I can give you a very simple example of an uncomplicated play situation. John has been playing by himself for quite some time with a toy car. He is simply talking to himself and manipulating the car. Is there a child anywhere who has not involved himself in this kind of simple, solitary activity? What are the learning possibilities for John in this situation? He can discover and learn concepts about *space*, such as high, low, around, far, near. He can discover and learn concepts about *speed*, such as fast, faster, slow, stop. He can discover and learn concepts about *direction*, such as forward, backward, left, right, up, down. At the same time he can practise and learn *sensory discrimination* from the sound and feel of the car, and he can learn how to coordinate his movements to make the car go as he pleases. He can identify with the role of a bus driver and act out his role. In doing this, he can practise, consolidate, and gain mastery over his vocabulary and concepts to do with cars, safety, policemen, and so on that this model of the real world would evoke for him. He can learn to direct himself, think for himself, solve his own problems, put his past knowledge to work, adjust to new experiences and learnings.

A casual observer would likely be fooled by the apparent simplicity of what John was doing. He was learning what no one could teach him. We must recognize that, while play can seem idle and aimless, what the child is really seeking is to discover the basic dimensions and physical operations of the actual world and learn its space-time properties and physical relationships. We must remember the child may be endlessly rehearsing and practising what will later become a directive in all his activities.

Play is a major achieving pattern of children. Look again at the very young child who will stack the rings on a post and then dump them off and do it again, varying the order, the colour, the size, repeating the play until he feels he has mastered it. The child repeats this pattern of attempt, practise, and mastery daily in his play, adding to the store of things he feels sure of and safe with, reducing the uncertainty of the large and often inconsistent adult world. Slowly he gains confidence to investigate novel or complex stimulation, as long as the safety of the established pattern can be returned to whenever he needs to feel secure in himself again. This is why it is wise to have familiar objects, experience-events, or routines surrounding the child before bringing him into a new situation. We must try to help the child make the same kind of transition from old to new he instinctively makes in his play experiences.

Play increases a child's creativity. I am specifically referring to the child's capacity to perform a task which requires ingenuity in formulating an answer that is not readily suggested by the materials themselves or by another person. If posed a problem, such as two planks of wood and a stone and a pond too wide to be crossed by either plank alone, the creative or ingenious child will find a way to use the materials to solve the problem. For many years educators have assumed that there is a high correlation between intellect and creativity; this, in fact, may be a spurious relationship. Recent research indicates that creativity is related to several factors other than intellect.[13] For the teacher this means it is impossible to assume that because a child is not particularly bright, he will not be very creative, and that therefore it is appropriate to provide fewer opportunities or less stimulation. It is interesting to note in this connection that for years teachers of the mentally retarded have been insisting that their students were in fact very creative in many ways, and have been patted on their heads rather patronizingly by those who have felt secure in their knowledge that only intelligent children are creative.[38]

Development of Social Relationships Through Child's Play

Play moves the child into more and more complicated social relationships. I will briefly outline these stages, for they indicate, simply and clearly, the development of play patterns.[31]

Solitary play is engaged in by the very young child in an egocentric fashion to satisfy his own immediate needs. It may appear that he plays with adults, but in reality he only takes what the adult gives him and makes use of it in a very solitary fashion. In the school system it is more likely to be observed in a nursery school or junior kindergarten than the higher grades. However, this is not to say that solitary play is never characteristic of the older child. Depending upon a child's previous social experiences and his temperament, a child may still be at the solitary stage of play at ages five and six. Similarly, depending upon the mood he is in, a child older than six years of age may engage in solitary play when he regards the other children as a hindrance to his own particular interests.

Solitary play evolves into *onlooker play*, where the child observes other children as they are playing but does not enter into their play. In nursery school or junior kindergarten it is quite common to see the onlooker moving from one group of children to another, yet always standing or sitting apart from each group — sometimes empty handed, more often clutching a soft toy as a security blanket, showing an interest in the ongoing play yet emotionally unprepared to take an active part. This changes into *parallel play*, where two or more children engage in similar if not identical pursuits with no exchange of any kind of genuine feeling or real sharing of goals or thoughts. The children will look at each other and deal with each other and seem to be involved in the same kind of play but without actually meeting in it. The child who has progressed socially to the stage of parallel play is still quite conspicuous in the junior kindergarten. Although he has moved from the passive role of onlooker to the active role of doer, he continues to be a social isolate. Psychologically, he is not yet a member of any group, although both his active stance and the physical proximity of his play to a group tend to belie his psychological isolation. However, he is simply sharing the same box of toys with a nearby group, and not participating in the group's play — not even through imitation. For instance, the group may be building a zoo with small blocks and toy animals, while the parallel player is using the same toys to build a farm.

Parallel play often changes quite quickly into *associative play*, where children play alongside each other but the individual child continues to be an isolate. They may talk or exchange ideas or toys, but each child really does what he wants to do, and borrows or lends toys in terms of how he sees his own needs and projects developing. Their behaviour is imitative, however, and suggests the beginning of psychological rapprochement in that they are not only sharing the same toys but also imitating each other's behaviour. The children may be playing railroad and may talk about it, but each one will want to build his own tracks and buildings and trains, rather than working jointly on the project. Like solitary play, onlooker, parallel, and associative stages of play are characteristic of the very young child and are more frequently observed at the four-year level. At the parallel and associative play stages, small blocks of all shapes and sizes, small cars, people, and animals for building one's own zoo, city, farm, etc. are particularly valuable in that they facilitate the transition from one stage to the other. For instance, the necessity of sharing a box of small blocks and toy props (animals, people, cars) tends to encourage the group's "drawing in" of the associative player or players, who, because of their imitative behaviour, are also building a zoo and so have play materials to contribute to the group's larger zoo.

Associative play is only a short step from *cooperative play*, which is what we adults think of as the ultimate in the social character of play. Cooperative play is play where the children are genuinely exchanging feelings and interacting. They have a sense of belonging to the play they are involved in and to the group. There is an underlying organization to their play at this point: If they are playing railroad, there is usually an assignment of roles, either voluntarily, by tacit agreement, or at the instigation of one child who may be older or more mature or just plain bossy. As a child interacts with other children in this way, he is testing his developing self through games, using the rules as a way of finding out how he stands in relationship to other children. He is learning to anticipate the intentions and expectations of other players; this is essential to all his further social relationships with people all ages. No human being can interact safely with others without some ability to predict what will be expected or desired from him in terms of actions, behaviours, or feelings; this ability is clearly and spontaneously learned through unstructured — or perhaps a better term is self-structured — play.

Cooperative play may be found in the junior kindergarten and primary grades where true group play, in the psychological sense, takes place. If given freedom of choice to pursue whatever activities they desire, children at this stage of development will fluctuate between selecting group and individual activities according to their mood. Opportunity should be available for sorting, ordering, arranging, and matching familiar objects such as buttons (all shapes, sizes, colours, and types), beads, jars and small bottles, prizes from popcorn or cereal, crayons, swatches of material, screws and nails, stamps, post cards, etc. Small block play is useful for stimulating construction activities. Through their manipulation, the child comes to know their properties and potential uses. The use of wet media (finger paint, water, wet sand, etc.) and the use of soft, yielding materials (Play-dough®, clay, etc.) afford the child an opportunity to fluctuate at will between group or individual play and exploratory or repetitive behaviour. Since each of these media involves no special skills on the child's part, the child can pour, pound, squeeze, roll the material without fear of failure.

Play can be considered as being composed of two major divisions: sensory-motor play and dramatic-symbolic play. Sensory-motor is the mode of play for the infant; as the child grows he will integrate it with dramatic-symbolic play.

There are a considerable number of activities which can be considered as sensory-motor play: grasping blocks, rolling balls, cutting things out, manipulating crayons or pencils, stacking toys, manoeuvering trucks, working with picture puzzles, climbing trees, rolling in the grass, collecting stones or twigs; in short, any activity in which the child is *receiving* information by *doing* something. This kind of play is really the beginning of the child's learning to use his arms, hands, legs, feet, and entire body. The child repeats a behaviour in an effort to learn and to integrate a particular kind of motor behaviour, either gross motor behaviour or that requiring fine muscular control, into the rest of his repertoire. Children involve themselves in sensory-motor play not just to integrate motor behaviour, but for the sheer joy of mastering situations, for the pleasure of showing off and displaying their mastery over their own body and over reality. The pleasure which comes from nearly effortless ability to perform a physical act requiring skill, coordination, and stamina keeps human beings involved most of their lives: golf, water skiing, bicycle riding, jogging, ballet, and tennis are only a few of the adult activities which display this continuing need for master evident in the young child.

Sensory-motor play also allows children to receive information about their physical and social environment and helps them to differentiate themselves from their non-selves. Essentially, this is how the whole concept of body image develops; this is the way the child evolves the idea of "Who am I, what can I do, where do I end and the rest of the world begin?" We see this beginning in the infant who finally gets his toes into his mouth and enjoys the feeling and sensation both on his toes and in his mouth, and we see it when the infant gets someone else's fingers into his mouth and slowly realizes there is a difference: the sensation is limited, and the child begins to sense that this finger does not belong to him in the same way as did the first things he nibbled on. As he grows, he elaborates this sensory-motor experimenting and begins to integrate this kind of information about the world of reality and himself.

Another element in sensory-motor play is learning to handle and manipulate materials: a child learns the multiple uses of materials and this encourages movement in the direction of new goals and permits him to assimilate new information. With the assimilation of this new information, he is able more easily to accommodate to the environment; this is what learning means for all humans.

Dramatic-symbolic play begins when the child begins to make use of make-believe and illusion in his playing. In dramatic play, the child tries to deal with things which frighten him and with things he really does not understand. What he is trying to do is to evolve the "as if" part of himself which will later help him to meet expectations and fulfil different roles, as well as enable him to understand why other people act the way they do towards him. Play allows him to deal with the "as if" situations without getting so involved that he has no way of extricating himself. He can then explore what it is like to be his sister or Superman. He plays "If I were a fireman (nurse, teacher, mummy, big brother), what would happen to me, what would I do and be like?" He can gain the temporary satisfaction of being a girl, being a mother, being a father, and gradually learn his own role of being a child and a boy in the family. By pretending, he finds out the kinds of roles adults have, and this will eventually evolve into an aspect of making a vocational choice for himself. At this point in his young life, I am not concerned with his vocational choice but with the curiosity about the world which is partly satisfied by the acting out of his fantasies, doubts, fears, and good times. He begins to use symbols, to be more abstract, less concrete. A hat or a bag or a mask or an empty box is endowed with some kind of identity, some kind of symbolism for the role he is playing. At this stage, children are not very literal: a dolly makes a little girl a mummy, whether or not it has any clothes to wear or hair that really grows or a fancy bed to sleep in, or even a name. These added attractions become more necessary to the child as she grows older and more realistic — however, once the identity or even the sex of a doll has been established, a child playing will almost never bother to change it to suit the current make-believe!

As this dramatic-symbolic play evolves, the child begins to use words and images: he will describe things, talk about things, and follow his own activities with what is almost a commentary. He creates representations of the events which concern him in his surroundings, and pretends, verbally, that they are there. He will then make use of these objects or events in a symbolic way of his own making for his own purposes.

For example, once I watched two children, ages three and five, who had been to see *The Nutcracker Suite* ballet at Christmas; for several weeks, the ballet kept popping up in their play. They would pretend to be various characters and pretend to put on costumes and makeup, dance, come to the pretend curtain and bow — all to music from a music box. Then they would be the characters before or after the ballet began, having a separate life. They had had difficulty understanding why the adults were not concerned with a mouse after it left the stage, supposedly injured, and kept asking where the mouse was, if it was in the hospital, or dead, or would it come back later? In their play they tried to solve this question, playing out various things that could happen to the mouse to explain why he did not enter the story again. All the time they talked and designated parts of the living room or available adults to fill needed roles as parts of the scenery or other dancers or audience, changing in mid-step from one dancer to the conductor or the mouse. Apparently they worked it out to their satisfaction, because eventually more familiar games like nursery school and helping mummy and visiting relatives came to the fore again.

The child must learn to use language symbolically in order to understand that a symbol or two in the form of a letter or letters represents a sound or combination of sounds which in turn form a word — in other words, to understand the concept of reading. When a child begins to use language in his play, then, it is important to encourage the seemingly pointless talking and explaining as the child talks about what he is doing. His language has to catch up with his actions: this is why, many times, we really do not understand what the child is saying, why his current actions do not match his current words. His ability to describe the present and then to differentiate it from the past and the future depends on his continuing use of symbolic language in his play; to a large measure, his future reading ability depends on this kind of play activity.[49]

No one should underestimate the power of dramatic play. Although it can take on many forms, Hartley[20] has pointed out eight basic functions:

to imitate adults
to play out real life roles in an intense way
to reflect relationships and experiences
to express pressing needs
to release socially unacceptable impulses
to reverse roles usually taken
to reflect and encourage changes in attitudes and adjustment
    to reality
to work out problems and experiment with solutions

These functions surround three general motifs which are

constants in children's dramatic play: a need for protection, a need for power, and a need to attack and destroy. Certainly these needs and the balancing of these needs against the expression of the powerful feelings involved are universal in children and adults alike, and one's acceptable adjustment to the realities of adult society requires learning an appropriate balance of impulse and activity. If through dramatic play children learn something about expressing these needs in a way both satisfactory to them and acceptable to society, they are learning something just as important to them as a cognitive skill, such as reading, and no doubt this learning will contribute to reading acquisition.

Imagination is the arena of play. This is where the child can begin to dramatize the function of airplanes, animals, vehicles, and people and where play helps to clear up some of the confusions of his day. Play allows the child to explore those aspects of the world and his imagination which are frightening to him. Play permits the child to do something with his thoughts. He cannot explore his thoughts if he is forced to do a reading lesson; even if pushed, the reading lesson does not advance because he is too engrossed in his thoughts.

But he *will* read after he has cleared up the confusions, which are more important to him than reading. Play allows this, and once accomplished, provides the inspiration and motivation for his reading, for the child will find the books and magazines which will serve his play.

CHAPTER 4

THE SPACE — AND THE PROPS TO FILL IT

THE environment of the child which is a learning environment is a responsive and appropriate one; one which must reflect the life of the child, become a natural setting within which he can continue his physical, intellectual, emotional, and social growth. The environment is a nurturing one to develop his competencies and skills; it is one which fulfills his natural desire to become an effective and important person in his world. The environment is free in that there is a freedom for him to design his own sequence in learning and to cope with problems as they arise. This is freedom of an appropriate nature, encouraged and guided and watched over by an understanding adult.

The appropriate environment provides opportunity for the child to use his sensory abilities, his cognitive abilities in terms of problem-solving, his motor abilities in terms of physical experimentation, and his language abilities in terms of verbal forms of communication. His learning depends on sensory experiences, and he acquires information by a multitude of experiences in his environment. These experiences are, in effect, led by or determined by interests and curiosity. The child explores, selects, builds, discovers, recreates, and repeats activities.

If we expect the child to make room for our concepts in his mind, then we must make room for him to acquire those concepts by giving him the space to work in. He cannot just sit at a desk and work; he needs to move. He cannot use fine motor movement like us, he needs to explore much more of his gross motor activities. He needs space to run in, to climb, to jump, to push, to roll, to do thousands of gross motor activities before he can be expected to sit and have an attention span at a desk.

In an effort to try and gain an understanding of their environment, children use activity as the basis for their mental construction of space. For instance, the child between the ages of three and five seems to conceive of space in terms of his physical actions. If he can do something, if he can run, jump, feel, move, then those aspects of action become incorporated into his comprehensive map. The comprehensive map becomes detailed as he becomes more involved for longer periods of time with specific actions. The spatial relationship that the child has of his area appears to be influenced by his capacity to move, touch, push, squeeze himself and objects within the space. Without this kind of sensory-motor activity, the child's capacity to perceive and organize his space into a cognitive, comprehensive map is limited, if not distorted. Naturally, then, if we allow gross movement in the classroom, then encourage "involvement time" or the space and time for detail work, the child will develop because we have provided the "mental space" for a development which is meaningful and organic to the child.[47]

Furthermore, the study of exploratory behaviour and play behaviour suggests that the child explores and then plays. When the child has examined the object so that it loses its foreign qualities, the child may either ignore it or incorporate it into his play. The child investigates a great number of situations and objects in this manner: he searches out and comes to terms with the strangeness of the object (as long as it is not too strange) and its spatial arrangement in the classroom, then, through the activity of play, incorporates these aspects into his cognitive mapping.

Thus, classrooms need space; they need central open areas where lots of activities can go on, activities needed by the developing child, such as walking, running, sitting, rolling, looking, climbing, holding, touching, and smelling. The child then needs "bays" where he can take the play material he has discovered and which has appealed to him, extend it in quietness, and make further discoveries.

When I speak of space I do not mean openness of architecture. It is neither necessary nor sufficient to self-discovery learning. Although many children are taught in modern schools without walls, good self-directed learning can occur just as easily within a conventional four-walled classroom. What is necessary is openness of mind — both of the teacher and of child. An imaginative teacher can take the conventional four-walled classroom and create an arrangement of furniture to provide ample spaciousness while managing to emphasize various learning centres. For example, tables and movable desks can be arranged singly or in groups to form work areas. Adjustable shelving on wheels can be used to partition off interest centres while serving as storage space for project work. Boxes of toys can be padded or covered with cushions to provide seating. Movable partitions made of tackboard can be acquired at little cost, yet provide extra display area for children's work.

The teacher's openness of mind is necessary for entertaining a positive attitude toward each child's capacity to make educationally relevant decisions with minimal teacher help. This, coupled with a well-directed sensitivity, can also work to help her see each child as a unique individual with his own particular learning history and pattern of acting and reacting, and so help her decide when a child cannot cope adequately with the usual amount of nondirectedness. If he can cope better in a more structured environment with fewer options open to him, then while still providing some choice she limits the activities from which he must choose. Yet like the other children, he makes his own choice of activity to pursue to its completion in consultation with the teacher, and so learns to cope with a measure of nondirectedness and to use it to grow toward disciplined endeavour, to develop a sense of self-responsibliity. The child must be able to observe and assess his actions, not only in relation to what he did before but also in relation to the model the teacher provides. It is one thing for the teacher to be continuously assessing the growth of the child, but it is another thing for the child to begin to recognize that he must assume some responsiblity for his action. If we ask the teacher to be the only assessor in the classroom, then we remove this vital aspect of self-responsibility from the child. For example, a five-year-old child with whom I was involved had considerable trouble relating to other children, continuously behaving in an infantile, demanding, and disorganized way. We were able to help her assess herself in one small area in the beginning. She was interested in plants, and together we worked out a sheet which she had tacked upon the wall indicating the day of the week by colour and name and a box below each day she was to fill in with the appropriate colour after having completed her plant-watering activity. She managed to do this, not without some trouble at first. Under the direction of the teacher, she completed several weeks of self-responsible behaviour — she was responsible for watering the plants and for recording her action on the chart. She was assessing her own behaviour, and it was gratifying to notice her take the chart off the wall and proudly show it to anyone who would look at it. She had completed a whole month and the chart was full, but it also looked like a beautiful coloured carpet!

On the child's part, an openness of mind is necessary as well — an openness toward his responsibility in the learning process. It is his responsibility to actively explore the classroom environment in the pursuit of knowledge and in the interest of self-development and to attune to changes in it. Further, it is his responsibility to search for, pursue, organize, and incorporate any new information in a multitude of ways by making combinations and recombinations of that information, to be flexible and adaptive in his approach to problem solving and to generate appropriate value judgments.

While I assign to the child these very significant responsibilities, I assign to educators and concerned adults the responsibility for providing the space and the learning materials which are needed if he is to fulfil his responsibilities. He needs to learn the properties of bulk and form; he needs to learn about space occupancy; he needs to learn concepts such as flow, up, down, around, heavy, light, and he will learn these if we provide the environment to help him.

What kind of materials, raw and ideational, best accomplish the learning through play? Should the materials be of the finished, polished variety, like dolls, trucks, dishes, or should they be of the raw variety, things like clay, paper, sand, tree bark, stones? What balance should there be between variety of materials, and when should the materials be used? These are questions to which there are no ready and easy answers. More study and experiment into the way children use their materials is needed: teachers need help in order to make use of their own skills at play and enable them to see the child's developing needs. The very young child will use clay as his creating material; some will move gradually, others quickly, into using paper and experiment in this medium. The teacher can help by having a sensitivity to the needs of the child and by being prepared to bring out materials at the appropriate times: not to stultify, not to over stimulate, but to move along at the developing rate of the child.[47]

Outside the classroom we often try too hard to provide the right materials. If we carefully watch young children playing in a backyard we will see them play through many learning processes with the material at hand. They develop communication using language which is relevant to them: their speech is brief with no long, drawn-out talks. There will be leadership encounters, either in a single pattern leadership or a multiple and changing leadership. Leadership stays until ideas are exhausted, or until the children move on to another area. They will play, using the materials of a backyard, pieces of chairs, bedsprings, glass, poles, cardboard, and wood. These pieces are fashioned into other objects: the chair becomes a bridge or the paper becomes a dress. The child is learning through play how to relate the objects to other uses, learning the dimensions of form, task involvement, even mathematics (when he has another piece of paper "as big as that one"). He learns through play how to interrelate the materials of the next child to his object and then how to make his own object either fit in with the other child's or make a new one for the next child.

He is learning social relationships. The children move in and out of the game. They add different aspects to it and then it alters. The child who cannot keep up, or wishes to play the game differently, either stays with his material or his game until he is ready to move on, or if he is threatened by the move, he may become the bully to preserve his safety.

I am only using the backyard scene because I think it teaches us that children need space — they bring their materials with them. Too often middle and upper socioeconomic playgrounds have too much equipment designed by some designer who thinks he knows how kids will make use of materials. Unfortunately he is often wrong and then the kids have to alter his work so they can play with it — they convert hardware into childware.

Math Centre

This backyard concept can be brought beautifully into the classroom. For instance, in relating mathematics to play, to materials and to knowledge, there are several ways to increase the ease of the child in learning number concepts and recognition. Tally and concept of sign can be provided by playing a game of catch and tallying the individual throws and catches; playing a game of telephone calling and tallying the number of calls that have been made and so forth. The child, given a pad and pencil, will tally just about anything that comes to hand! As he tallies and counts to reach a total, he is talking to other kids and to the teacher, learning how to relate in a language way the numbers and number concepts he is learning. He imitates other children and the teacher as well. At this point, he is ready for a number line, a simple chart built up in equal units to show how many catches he made today, yesterday, the day before; how many telephone calls he made yesterday and today, and how many days have gone by this week.

Next comes recognition of numbers, which the teacher can facilitate by setting up the classroom so that the child becomes aware of the different numerals. For example, she may have a calendar on which she circles today's date, or she counts the days on a pad until the arrival of special events, or a clock on which hands can be set for special times (like recess or lunch) for the children to compare with the real clock.

The teacher needs also to set up learning bays where the children can experiment in meaningful ways with meaningful numbers. The *store* is about the best way to acquire number concepts. The child can buy from the store, sell to his peers, make change, and keep records of the transactions. He learns number recognition when another child asks how much something costs; he learns addition and subtraction by making change; he learns the concepts that go with terms like more than, greater than, less than. He learns how to print out what the store sells and how much it costs. He helps others to read because they ask what he has to sell. He is travelling in learning at his own speed with the ready help of the teacher and other children.

Another effective piece of equipment for understanding numbers is the *weighing machine.* The child weighs objects and records numbers, he compares weights of various objects and begins to understand the relationship of volume to weight because he fills containers with sand, water, pebbles, acorns, or sticks and weighs them. He begins to find out the difference between heavy and light, big and small and smaller, all in a context which is meaningful to him.

As he makes use of these games and materials he is learning to write numbers because they are meaningful and necessary to him in his work, rather than because someone wants him to copy them out in a book. He is learning verbal concepts, such as one more, one less, heavier than, bigger than, in a way that makes sense to him because he has used them in his play. The teacher is there to direct, ask questions, and extend his thinking and play so that he begins to learn concepts that are quite complicated, such as things weighing the same although they are of different sizes. He is stimulated to explore and experiment when he comes upon an occurrence or event he does not immediately grasp. Soon the child is ready to make use of games which require math — he can play with dice or dominoes, keep track of scores in snakes and ladders, and play bingo.

In this math centre, the child can explore geometric shapes and explore his sense of abstract. He should be encouraged to explore the classroom and outdoors for shapes everywhere. In terms of materials he will need solid shapes to manipulate — blocks, sugar cubes, beads, prisms, boxes, cans, tubes, and so on.

Young children can make a family picture paperweight

(cube) by covering each side of a square box with a photo (or crayon picture) of family members; they can make a shape booklet, hand-drawn or cut from magazines; and they can use various geometrically shaped cookie cutters with Play-doh. The teacher can organize a shape centre with one shape featured each week until all geometric shapes are covered. Then they can move to examining symmetry. Children can tramp geometric shapes in the snow — ball diamond, fox and geese circle, four and twenty blackbirds baked in a pie, boxing ring.

After manipulation of solid geometric figures, young children can use peg boards with elastic around the outside of strategically placed pegs to make various shapes. If nails and wood are used, outlining the nails with brightly coloured yarn and varnishing the wood makes a nice wall hanging. Younger and older students alike enjoy using various shapes in their box sculptures and mobiles. Older students can cast various shapes by pouring plaster of paris into shaped wet sand. These moulds can be painted. Round moulds can be painted for Halloween masks.

I was observing a group of children in a grade 1 and 2 classroom — the school operates on the project basis, and on this particular day the children were going to study arithmetical concepts. The teacher, who was working with twenty-one children, talked with them as they sat in a circle around her. She explained that they were going to use paper, pencils, long pieces of narrow wood, string, scissors, and glue, and that the project would be "trying to find out how tall each child was."

Some of the children began to stand against the wall holding their hands at the spot where their head touched the wall. They quickly discovered they needed a pencil to mark the spot, or another child to note it. Some children lay on the floor and quickly noted they needed two reference points, so some moved to the wall and placed their feet at the baseboard. These children also noted the need for help or for a pencil. The activity proceeded with a great deal of manipulation of materials, with much verbal exchange and, gradually, as the playing with materials continued, the following experience evolved.

Some children had tied the narrow strips of wood together

and fashioned rulers and were measuring each other. Since the pieces of wood had no markings, the children made their own markings by taking a very small piece of wood and marking the larger pieces with the small one as a standard and then by simply counting standard units they evolved a scale for measuring. As they wrote down the numbers, noting that some were smaller than others, one child suggested grouping the numbers and rather quickly the concept of graphing evolved. It was crude at first, it simply showed how many children were the same height, but the sheets changed when one child suggested they use squares, one on top of another to indicate the number of children of the same height.

I believe that this concept of learning is fairly standard now in many classrooms. When the child is given the opportunity to play with the materials, to find out how they work, what can be done with them, how they can be used, the child manipulates those materials in many ways, always learning as he does and never feeling constrained by the materials themselves. He forces the materials to work for him, he does not stop when the materials seem to stop. The teacher did not give instructions for each medium, she told the children the media available and what the project was; she was available to the children and encouraged them in their play. She did not restrict them by indicating the restrictions of the materials, for who knows but perhaps a child may come up with a way of working the media which we do not know of as yet. Premature restrictions and instruction inhibits the use of materials and the learning of concepts. Restrictions enforce a kind of closure which is inadequate and does not allow the child to move forward in his activities.

Something else happened with some of these children. A small group of five children noted that two sides of a triangle were fashioned when one child stood at the wall and the other child lay on the floor at the base of the wall. What they did was to mark the spots with chalk, then string a cord from the two far ends. They did this with several combinations and began to notice that the hypotenuse of this right-angled triangle varied as a result of the lengths of the two sides, i.e. the height of the two children. They started to graph this variation in hypotenuse and side and while no conclusions were reached, they had not only entered the field of graphs and measurement but had started into geometry!

By the way, these kids were sufficiently interested in triangles that they began to build models of wood and discovered different kinds of triangles and some of their properties.

A math centre in the classroom can accomplish all this and more without once resorting to a desk-and-copying situation. Other areas of classroom learning can be treated in exactly the same manner.

Communication Centres

There can be *a book centre*, where a variety of books and magazines form a collection for recreational reading and research activities. Nearby, yet away from the flow of traffic to the centre, should be a quiet spot for reading, furnished with carpet, easy chair, and cushions. Also in the same general area, there can be *a listening centre*, containing a collection of tapes and records to be heard over earphones, some of which are made by the children, others purely recreational, while still others foster reading skills, and *a viewing centre*, where filmstrips are available for browsing or for research activities.

The *dramatization centre* needs a variety of materials to permit the acting out of roles of the real and the imagined: the role of the classroom visitor such as the policeman or the school nurse, the daily lives of people in other countries, the life of a television hero, the lives of animals.

The *communication centre* is the hub of the classroom; the focus here is not only to encourage the children to write about their experiences, hopes and fantasies, but also to help them to do so. To this end, the following equipment should be accessible: a typewriter, blackboard, a variety of dictionaries, lists of frequently encountered words grouped under such diverse categories as colours, textures, shapes, sizes, opposites, synonyms, action words, cities, television characters and programs, television guide, community helpers, countries, continents, animals, automobiles, etc.

Man communicates through listening, speaking, reading, and writing. Kindergarten children begin school at different levels in each of these areas. For example, the kind of listening a young child does is dependent upon the way he has been spoken to, and the kind of speaking he does is dependent upon the models he has had and the respect that has been shown his ideas. The child who has received little attention will be at a disadvantage when it comes to listening attentively and expressing his ideas effectively. Similarly, some children arrive at school at more advanced levels in the reading and writing areas. The communication centre, therefore must be arranged to cater to these individual variations in communication skills.

Although the speaking and writing of good English is a major aim, to arrive at it by demanding correct spelling and punctuation at the expense of the expression of the children's thoughts and feelings is certainly to go down in defeat. Children should be encouraged to use correct spelling and punctuation by having all kinds of dictionaries, plus prepared lists of frequently met words, available at the communication centre. However, to red pencil spelling or punctuation errors is to be frowned upon. Minicentres of interest should be set so as to encourage the communication of ideas in listening, speaking, reading, and writing. With older children, the use of codes (Morse code, flags, hand signals, sign language) and braille are of particular fascination.

There is an endless list of activities basic to development of communication, all geared to the personal reality of the child. They can write invitations to classroom visitors (principal, parents etc.), write a letter to Santa Claus, and write thank-you notes; develop and write down classroom obligations, write lists of groceries for the doll centre, use a food dictionary with pictures of food pasted beside the printed name. Children can make use of real (preferably) or toy telephones to order groceries for the housekeeping centre from the play store and phone the police station, drug store, fire department, grandmother, doctor, etc. Children can read the *T.V. Guide* and sort programs according to "my favourites," westerns, cartoons, musicals, and so forth. The results can be graphed or illustrated with pictures on a large mural. The children can investigate alternative methods of communication by learning about flag signals from a senior Boy Scout or Leader and practise illustrating the signals; make a telegraph key and send Morse Code signals; invite a blind visitor to show and read Braille, then send a thank-you note in Braille. Children can create their own mock T.V. studio, construct a set complete with microphone, and use it to practise oral communication (phone-in show, talk show) with topics to be discussed of immediate interest to them: "Are there too many school rules or not enough?"

They can simulate a newscast or sportscast to practise oral reading skills. The writing of free verse releases the child to express his feelings.

Activities can be organized to lead the child into the skills of understanding of language:

a. matching games
b. following command games
c. guessing games
d. using objects in the various mini-interest centres to sort into various categories: animals, pets, toys, textures, helpers, vegetables, tastes, and so on. Sorting and talking about them can lead to considerable development and vocabulary growth: *animals* (wild or tame; fierce, gentle, etc.); *material* (smooth or rough; velvety, knubby, gritty, soft); *people* (grownups, adults; or children; creep, crawl, cranky, strong, weak, gurgle),
e. solving (writing own) crossword puzzles
f. illustrating synonyms, antonyms, homonyms; keeping own synonym booklet

Further activities will lead the child into a deeper understanding of language and should include using contextual clues, pantomime, signals, finding main idea of a paragraph, story, poem, paraphrasing:

a. retelling or rewriting a story from the point of view of one character
b. study of distress signals, e.g. ship, airplane, animal
c. pantomiming bouncing a ball, pumping up a tire, walking

a tightrope
d. finding the main idea of a story and then writing another story using the same idea
e. paraphrasing a nursery rhyme
f. writing and guessing riddles
g. exchanging "Surprise Booklets" with a friend. Each child prepares a booklet by pasting articles (perhaps a feather), pictures (from magazine, a postcard, or a snapshot), single words (spooky) — one to a page. He then exchanges the booklet with a friend who writes something on each page. It may be a description of the article or picture, or an expression of how it makes him feel, or what it could be used for, etc. Where single words are written the child may try to surprise his friend by writing an interesting story. When finished, the booklet is given back to the original owner. Later, it may be passed around the room.

To teach children the concept of sequence, that is, the following of one word after another, one sentence after another, one thought after another, you can set up an oral discussion or pictorial illustration of events, which can then be cut up and reordered into correct sequence:

a. go through steps in a recipe (making cookies, Jello®, Kool-Aid®)
b. steps in getting ready for school, bed, etc.
c. steps in sending a letter (to Santa Claus)
d. steps in preparation for class trip
e. sequence of events in favourite story, poem
f. putting cut-up cartoon strips into correct sequence
g. write own cartoon strips to cut up for other students to sequence
h. visits to new building going up, to observe and record sequence

Art Centres

The art centre includes multiple materials for self-expression, such as chalk, clay, Play-doh, paint, felt pens, finger paint, papier-mâché, crayons, construction paper, scissors, glue, cellophane tape, thumb tacks, stapler, etc. With young children (kindergarten and grade 1), it is preferable to arrange two art centres, one for the wet and messy media and one for the dry. Various tools, such as tart trays, plastic dishes and cutlery, rollers, cookie cutters, etc., should be available for use with Play-doh and clay. A *treasure box* containing various odds and ends, such as scraps of wallpaper, feathers, polystyrene, blocks, material, ribbons, string, yarn, cork, wood scraps, straws, cardboard, rolls, buttons, beads, wire scraps, and small dowels, should be available close to the art centre. A series of mini-centres crop up around the art centre:

The *dry sand centre* has a tray of fine sand and varied small toys — small animals, airplanes, fences, scenic material, houses, barns, people, cars, street signs, etc. — available which can be used to arrange real or imaginary environments such as zoos, farms, cities, streets. Spades, rakes, and many plastic containers of all sizes should be available for digging and dumping purposes.

The *wet sand centre* has wet sand and multiple tools and utensils available for digging, scooping, moulding, and sculpting — spoons, spades, spatulas, scoops, plastic containers, toy dishes, tart trays, cookie cutters, egg cups, gelatine moulds, etc.

The *water play centre* should have a water tray large enough for three or four children to work around at one time. A small amount of dye and liquid soap can be added. Various containers for pouring and measuring should be available, such as measuring cups and spoons, plastic containers of a variety of shapes and sizes, funnels, basters, sieves, etc. A further ingenious use of materials can be used to encourage experimentation leading to self-discovered "facts."

a. water pressure: cans with holes punched in the sides at varying levels, plastic straws, and tubing of various diameters
b. the discovery and classifying of objects into float and non-float categories using sponges and cork, plastic, wood or metal, and rubber objects familiar to children
c. bubble blowing through the use of toy bubble pipes and

wire rings of various shapes and sizes

d. filtering: use of filter or blotting paper to ascertain whether dyed, sandy, salty, sugared water can be filtered
e. experiments with volume
f. experiments with water displacement

The *carpentry centre* is a work bench where tools such as pliers, wrenches, screwdrivers, planes, hammers, squares, rulers, etc. are available, as well as nails, screws, glue, and pieces of wood.

The *large block centre* is where large wooden blocks and various length planks are available so that children can build large-scale models of trains, buses, ships, airplanes, rocket ships. Since these large-scale models often develop in cooperation with the play activities of the housekeeping centre, it is advisable that this centre be adjacent to it.

Housekeeping Centre

In the housekeeping centre the children can practise playing the roles of family members, television heroes, community helpers, etc. Equipment should include toy kitchen stove and refrigerator; dishes, cutlery, and utensils; table and chairs; blankets; dolls and doll clothes, doll carriage; telephone, stuffed toys; a long mirror, and a variety of props to be brought out at appropriate times — such as male and female (adult and child) wearing apparel, costumes, caps and hats (fireman's, policeman's, bus driver's, ship captain's, conductor's, chef's, sailor's, nurse's, doctor's, etc.), fire hoses, doctor's kits, walking canes, crutches, umbrella, wigs, hair rollers, hand mirror, handmade signs, etc. For nursery and kindergarten children a life-sized baby doll which allows the children to practise dressing and undressing, working zippers, buttoning up, putting on shoes, tying bows and shoe laces, etc. is important for the encouragement of self-sufficiency and self-responsibility.

Music Centre

In the music centre a variety of instruments are useful for

experimentation and enjoyment of rhythm and sound — string instruments to pluck at different levels of tautness, percussion instruments for exploration of rhythm. Making one's own instruments is to be encouraged. For example, making wooden blocks covered with sandpaper; maracas out of plastic containers or boxes filled with rice, beans, or corn; drums made from coffee cans covered with tightly stretched rubber, etc. Children can experiment also with tonal patterns by arranging and rearranging a collection of bottles filled to different levels with water. If various colours of food colouring are added to each bottle to distinguish them, children can use colour coding to write their own music.

Sensory Centres

Infiltrated with all these major and mini centres are a series of *multisense centres* where children contribute objects from home so they can learn not only to develop their senses but also to apply appropriate adjectives to describe various sensations.

In the *taste centre,* foods are brought and cut into small pieces or placed in small plastic containers so that children can learn to distinguish such tastes as sour, sweet, bland, spicy, bitter. Vegetables, fruits, Jello powders, dehydrated soups, flour, baking soda, chocolate, cocoa, and coconut are just a few of the many possibilities.

In the *touch centre,* a "touch bag," that is, a drawstring bag into which the child can insert his hand, can serve as a handy means to encourage children to explore and try to name objects simply through touch. Objects of such varied textures as rough, smooth, bumpy, soft, etc., should be part of this centre.

In the *smell centre,* a variety of cooking materials such as coffee, tea, fruit juices, garlic, vinegars, spices, dehydrated foods, Jello powders, etc., can be placed in concealed containers so that the sense of smell becomes important for discovering what is inside.

There are as many *sight centres* possible as teacher and children have ideas; for example, a *colour centre* wherein one colour is featured at a time, such as white. Here, such diverse objects can be brought from home and handled, labelled, usage discussed, classified, etc., as flour, baking soda, baking powder, bread, cauliflower, onion, salt, nurse's cap, policeman's glove, shoe polish, baby's shoe, etc.

A *shape centre* (discussed earlier) is where one shape is featured at a time. When "round" is featured, one might find contributed an orange, apple, cookie, pie plate, car wheel, jar ring, etc.

A *picture centre* should be available where pictures from magazines, calendars, slides, postcards, hockey cards, etc., can be viewed and enjoyed, described orally and written about, sorted and arranged according to such diverse categories as mountain scenery, water scenes, rural or urban, native or foreign, cultures, people or places, and so on. The children should be encouraged to develop their own system of categorization. This centre can arouse specific interests, and so lead to a variety of projects: the study of a specific culture, the comparison of cultures (eastern and western), to a study of volcanoes, mountain ranges, forms of transportation.

Like the sight centre, the possibilities for *sound centres* are unlimited. For example, various sounds can be taped by individuals or by groups to be shared by others — animal noises, crickets chirping, frogs croaking, the roar of a waterfall, television commercials, students from a neighbouring classroom singing a special song, the senior band, particular musical instruments, traffic noises, the school bell, a fire siren.

In the *puppet show centre* puppets are available for impromptu and practised playlets. Child-made puppets (paper bag, stick, cloth, and sock) are to be encouraged. Backdrops can be painted, dialogue written, playlets videotaped.

Although lack of space of itself would prohibit the operation of all of these learning centres at any one period of time, common sense, too, would suggest that too many centres of interest would afford more stimuli than most young children could adequately handle. As a rule, certain learning centres are established as ongoing centres throughout the school year, while others are of a more temporary nature. Which centres should be permanent, and which should be temporary, depends on the ages of the children.

Schools in our major cities no longer give art, music, and movement or dance "frill" status. They are beginning to realize each is a worthwhile educational experience and should be treated accordingly in the curriculum. Just as in the area of constructive skills (what we call learning skills), the effective teacher of art, music, and movement must receive training in child development. Indeed, good training is imperative, for the teacher must be knowledgable not only about how children develop cognitively in these areas of self-expression but also how their cognitive growth is related to their emotional health and visual-motor-spatial development. Once aware of this interrelationship, the teacher's role becomes that of a resource person trained to arrange the environment so as to provide time and space for active experimentation, and a climate of interest and acceptance.

During the critical period of development in the young child's life, when he is using his graphic skills to first experiment at random with putting his impressions on paper (the "scribble" stage mentioned in Chapter 2), and later, to translate these into symbol expression (preschematic), certain conditions must be met if creativity, cognitive growth, and emotional health are to be realized. First, there is no room for an environment built on prevention (Johnny, don't spill the paints!) or convention (This is how to draw a house). Teacher-help should come in the form of questioning, not patterning. Second, a wide variety of experiences from which to draw for self-expression are necessary. To this end, the teacher's role becomes that of extending the child's conception of reality — objects and events — inside the classroom by asking questions designed to encourage an examination of objects and situations from a variety of perspectives and by reading good literature and outside the classroom by going on exploratory trips (or short walking trips or a bus ride) such as a trip to the market or zoo, to see, hear, and smell this new environment.

Third, a wide variety of media should be available which can meet the child's interest in form and colour yet provide both ease of manipulation and success.[8] Media such as finger paints,

Play-doh, clay, chalk, collage, paper and paste, boxes for box sculpture and mobiles, scraps of wood for woodworking, paint, and crayons should be available for exploration and experimentation. Fourth, an awareness on the part of the teacher of the difference between repetition to achieve mastery and stereotype due to emotional rigidity is a requisite. Fifth, at all times self-expression, not picture-making and mastery over media, (not end products), are the main objectives. To this end, sensitivity on the part of the teacher to each child's stage of development, as well as appreciation of his efforts, is imperative.

Just as the teacher of the young child needs to be well trained in child development in artistic expression, she needs to be equally well-versed in the developmental aspects of movement and music. As in the area of artistic expression, the teacher's role in movement becomes that of providing rich experiences, space, and time for experimentation in an appreciative atmosphere. Too many teachers of young children err by placing major emphasis on achievement of skills rather than on the wealth of experience movement, with or without musical accompaniment, affords for creative expression, and social, emotional and sensory-motor growth.

A wealth of movement materials — trips, toys, storybooks, poems, records — are readily at hand as golden nuggets of expression to be mined and later refined. For example, a clown puppet or marionette can be used first to explore whole body actions: "be a happy clown, be a sad clown, put on clown shoes and move like a clown." Later, this same image can be used to explore and coordinate bodily parts in a new relationship: "clown with feet off the floor, clown with feet above his head." Also the child can discover and combine creatively the two qualities of movement: (1) *time* — sudden (darting, using whole body or isolated bodily parts) versus prolonged (sinking, melting, oozing, stretching) and (2) *force* — strong (firm stepping and jumping), light (touching the floor with fingers, feet, toes).

From a social-emotional viewpoint, movement to music may even serve to soothe the hyperactive and the hostile, aggressive child or to cause the anxious, inhibited child to become more assertive. It is imperative that every child be given the freedom and encouragement to explore the music for personal meaning, not only to foster creativity but also to allow him to bring to the movement that which is emotionally satisfying. An impulsive and demanding four-year-old can *be* a "mean old Mother Bear" without hurting anyone.

Even toddlers in the nursery school enjoy movement, whether in response to direct suggestion (Let's all be the giant. Everyone be the giant in his own way) or in response to musical accompaniment. The children's natural movements and experiences should be used and built upon; that is, walking, running, skipping, hopping, bouncing, falling, flying, etc. From these spontaneous movements, both a feeling for form and a vocabulary of whole bodily action will arise and gradually become extended to include in the kindergarten such movement forms and words as swooping, creeping, collapsing, freezing, stealing, leaping, sinking, exploding, slithering, etc.

Since each part of the body has a role specific to it to play in movement — *step* (feet), *carriage* (trunk), and *gesture* (hands and head) — movement is an important means of promoting body imagery through discovery of bodily parts and their coordination in creative expression. Older children can experiment with communicating through movement: meeting and parting, meeting and passing, meeting and joining.

Creative movement can be accompanied by rhythmic music or simply by percussion instruments or the teacher's voice, or both. Percussion instruments, such as a drum, tambourine, cymbals (sustained or prolonged time), and maracas (sudden time), afford rhythmic accompaniment plus teacher-movement which the use of a phonograph denies.

As in the evaluation of artistic creation through manipulation of art materials, evaluation in creative movement must focus on process and mastery of the medium rather than on a polished performance. The teacher must give up any preconceived ideas she might hold about appropriate movement if she is to receive the child's message. Comments which focus on the feeling aspect of the message, such as "We could *feel* your strength as you stepped so firmly and held your head so high" and "we could *feel* your sadness in your plodding step and drooping shoulders" can help a teacher overcome preconceived ideas of "accurate" movement.

We must realize that not only must we provide the space and the appropriate things to put in it to encourage play, we must also provide the emotional atmosphere wherein a child can discover, make mistakes, change them, and go on to acquire principles, in short, an atmosphere which allows for learning. The teacher in such a classroom provides guidelines and safety (which sometimes means instruction), then the child can use the materials and space in an innovative, creative way.

CHAPTER 5

THE TEACHER'S ROLE

The one essential point in the whole educational system is the point of contact between teacher and child. It is to make this contact as fruitful as possible that everything else — authority, administration, inspection, curriculum — exist. If the system fails to work at this point of contact, it fails everywhere. But the contact is a personal one. It is a contact between persons, and both the teacher and the pupil must have full scope as persons. If the teacher becomes simply a transmitter of other people's ideas and is obliged to follow a scheme of work thought out by somebody else, he ceases to act as a person, because he has not been made, or even allowed, to use his own mind and imagination, to the full extent. (John Blackie in *The Character and Aims of British Primary Education*.)

THIS is a beautiful statement on the aims, the ideals of an educational system. Blackie continues, stating that the aims of the English system are to allow, and actively encourage, each child to develop his full powers of body and mind (understanding, discrimination, imagination, creation) and to grow up as a balanced individual, able to take his place in society and to live "in love and charity with all men." In this system, the school is thought of not as the lowest outpost of a far-flung bureaucracy, but as an environment for children and teachers.

The authoritarian role of the British school teacher of a decade ago has given way to that of a facilitator, a consultant, a resource person. The teacher rarely meets with a large group of children at once; he or she moves around from child to child, small group to small group, listening, observing, suggesting, leading, questioning, stimulating. She helps channel the children's enthusiasms and energies to make full use of the carefully organized school space, indoors and outdoors. She helps children find where to look, who to go to, how to cope with the environment of the class; she encourages self-discipline and sets high standards for individual achievement through meaningful relationships with each child as a total person. A great deal of organization, self-control, and perspective is required of the teacher in terms of thinking out, preparing, evaluating, finding and making available materials and directions for all children, and yet fostering the interests and capacities of each one. As no report cards are issued, the teacher must keep abreast of each child's total development so he can be discussed with the headmaster and the parents. The teacher needs the ability to adjust, to be flexible, to learn from the children, to think on her feet. Frequent in-service training, good support from other teachers and the headmaster, and about five years of experience in this kind of setting seems to be required for a teacher to cope and grow.

Another aspect of the teacher's role in this atmosphere is honesty in her feelings for the children; feelings of annoyance, of concern, or even anger are not concealed; she reacts as a human being with other human beings. She is thus more responsive, more open to the children's feelings and needs.

Maybe part of the secret is that the fine teachers who create the successful British schools view as people the children with whom they work, and treat them accordingly, rather than viewing them as *pupils* (a gruesome word), a sort of third-class noncitizen who may achieve "peopleness" after an ordained number of years of proper humility achieved through strict discipline. They like children as people and enjoy being with them, and grow and expand as people themselves through their experiences with the children.

The British experience is not our experience: Their history, both culturally and educationally, has not been ours; their current lifestyle has a different flavour from ours. It is important to keep this in mind as we wistfully imagine a direct transplant to our soil. But underlining the successful British system is a concept of humanity and respect for the individual that we cannot ignore. We forget, in our anxiety over acquiring knowledge that is fixed with a beginning and an end and is full of facts, that we do, indeed, have the raw material with which to create an individual able to live "in love and charity with all men." We can no longer slough this off as philosophical idealism impractical to North American society.[45]

When I think of the teacher in our system, I think of a person who literally creates the environment in which the child can continue to develop the growing awareness of himself. The teacher, to me, is an observing person, one who is able to express spontaneity and creativity without imposing either of these characteristics on the child she is working with. The teacher is a planning person, one who is living in a learning environment. Learning and teaching, then, is a process of learning oneself. In the process of this learning, a quality of humanness and sensitivity is developed without the desire to always be right; for the teacher comes to realize that situations change, information alters previously know facts and the teacher is not always right.

Guidance, not interference; criticism, not punitiveness; humanness, not mechanicalness — these are the teaching tools of a system truly dedicated to the teaching of children.

I see in the educational model a need to shift from content rigidity to content openness, not only as a need for children but also for the teacher. It is no wonder that teachers who are forced by their role to remain static often leave teaching or become hardened; there is little satisfaction in teaching someone else's facts by someone else's rules, rules which too often have precluded a relationship of any meaning between student and teacher.

When the play-project-oriented teacher and child first meet they must begin to build a relationship with each other; the onus is on the teacher, as she is the one with the experience and training to initiate it. She does this by offering an experience for the child which is meaningful and within the already learned context of his self. In other words, the teacher finds an activity that the child can relate to easily and well and is not in any sense strange to his environment. Animals, food, junk material permit such a relationship to evolve. The teacher helps the child, if the child needs help, to begin to make choices. Thus, by providing the environment with certain activities which are well within the readiness level of the child, the teacher observes the capacity of the child to make decisions and choices. Some children will be able to choose immediately; others will not. The teacher is sensitive to the very unique and particular needs of each child in her class.

In an enlightened method of teaching children through self-discovery and play, the teacher understands that it must no longer be one person who knows it all and another who learns, but rather one person who guides and two people who learn — the teacher and the child. The two people learn because they recognize the individual differences between them and they transmit an understanding of this to each other, thereby acquiring a kind of personal discipline and control which is really part of the self-identity. Thus discipline is not imposed but comes from within in recognition of differences, through judgment and comprehension.

The relationship between child and teacher sharpens the child's self-awareness and helps him to recognize the differences between himself and his peers, the kinds of information he does not have, and to explore these areas, rather than backing off in fear of his ineptitude. If others value him he values himself; he need not be discouraged but can move from one level of competence to another, changing his self-picture, safe in the acceptance he feels from his teacher. There is no clash between what he is supposed to do and what he can do; the teacher recognizes and understands his development. She gives him the freedom to explore, allowing him to find out ways of knowing things.

This kind of a teacher recognizes that it is the individual child who is important, not the system. She knows that there is not a particular method to teach children, but rather many ways of approaching a child; one system does not work for all children. The child's social role, as well as his self-identity, evolves through his relationship with the teacher and through exploration; it is not ascribed to him in advance since the teacher does not see the system as the most important aspect of the environment.

The enlightened teacher blurs subject areas and single areas do not really exist any longer; information in one area is most certainly useful to information in another. During the first years in school, something as seemingly innocuous as block-building demonstrates this connection between hitherto separated areas, as well as showing again how essential play is to the learning child. The teacher in introducing the child to the blocks realizes that the growth of the child, not architectural masterpieces, is the first goal; physical release and body coordination as well as emotional release through the dramatic use of blocks are involved. At first the child may work alone, enjoying the success of creating a bridge or building; he may or may not want to talk about what he is doing. Later he begins to combine block and other play materials such as cars or trucks or clay or sand or water, basing his dramatic play on the setting he thereby creates. He may build a train station, for example, and then take imaginary trips either by himself or with others. He expands to take into account what those around him are building, perhaps working cooperatively to build a village. He may bring in materials or make things in other areas of the room, such as clay animals or paper cut-outs or paintings, to add to his creation.

Physics would not have evolved if not for mathematics; mathematics was certainly aided by the development of physics. If we think of such subjects as geology and biology as open content subjects, as for example, earth sciences, then we can begin to explore rational concepts of ecological principles. We can explore genetic change in environment. Why, where, how does this happen?

It is important to realize that in this model the teacher does not simply say "Let's do anything we want." In this teacher-child relationship, I do not suggest the teacher has no expectations for the child, or that goals are not set, nor do I mean the school is a free, permissive environment. Rather, the teacher respects the child's intelligence, integrity, creativity, and capacity for thought and hard work. There is an expectation, one that is often satisfied if held. I do know that when a teacher believes a child *cannot* perform, unfortunately the child usually fulfills that expectation. So I ask of our teachers that they set their expectations at a positive level. Such a teacher becomes recognized by the children as a person who does have standards and expectations. But while models of excellence and achievement are being sought for in each class, each child is encouraged to advance to the level of his developmental capacity. The child is not in competition with his peers or his teacher but is trying to achieve because of the motivating relationship that has been set into motion between himself and the teacher. The child will begin to measure himself against himself. Failure is not present and is not an obstacle to learning. The child's play and his project may be criticized, but he is helped by his teacher and his peers; he is not failed. The kinds of questions his teacher has asked him will encourage him to recognize the difficulties he has encountered and therefore enable him to formulate a new plan for his play which will allow him to develop and increase his learning.[51]

Assessment of the results of this teaching relationship with the child is not achieved by paper and pencil tests, which only control the content and direction of the curriculum, but rather by observing the child and finding out *what* he has acquired, *how* he has acquired the information, and whether he is ready to have his environment changed so as to help him acquire new and perhaps more complicated information. Undoubtedly, assessment by standard achievement tests is simpler, but it denies that children learn differently and at different rates one from another, and it denies the importance of everything the child learns that is not measured by that particular paper and pencil test.

The assessment is made by observation. The teacher observes the child daily, and sees what he is doing, comparing what he does today with what he did last week. The teacher then can set the environment so that the child can become involved in activity which encourages new learning experiences. Evaluation of progress has been made, but not in such a way that the child's activity has been limited. The child needs to experience success and change in order to continue his drive and desire to learn. Success comes because the teacher has observed what he needs to emphasize through emerging ideas. The relationship acts as the growing edge to learning and the desire to learn.

The exploratory classroom has flexibility. The child does not just stay in a group but is permitted and encouraged to go from group to small group. I think of these as teaching groups although they may not have the teacher with them at times. One of the children may assume the role of teacher, which indicates that the child has a certain confidence in himself and understands the material well enough to talk about it without the fear of argument from other children. This imitational role is incorporated into the growing self-picture.

Careful observation of children's impromptu dramatizations can afford the sensitive teacher much information about their fears, interests, and general knowledge. Many times the child's dramatic play can be original, spontaneous, and without teacher-preassigned roles; young children will come together without previously designed reason and then spontaneously evolve a dramatic play. One child takes on the role of a parent, another the role of a teacher, while yet another decides to be the baby. I was watching children in a classroom at play where this *dramatis personae* had spontaneously been arrived at. The play then moved into the realm of trying to find out why the child was not sucking the baby bottle. The child who was the parent complained to the teacher that the baby would not suck; the teacher asked was the nipple hole big enough; the mother said, yes, that she had tried to suck from the bottle and then, demonstrating with an imaginary bottle, began to show that she could suck the contents. The teacher and the mother looked at each other in a puzzled way, really simulating adult-kind-of-concentration. Then the mother asked the teacher "maybe the baby cannot suck?" To me this was really a startling question but I think the answer was even more startling. The teacher, with a look of concern and wisdom replied "maybe your baby is frightened." The mother went over to the baby, patted her, touched her, and made cuddling comments to her like "there, there, you're a nice baby, don't be afraid, we love you," and the baby responded. The baby took the imaginary bottle and started vigorously sucking.

To me this small dramatic play evidenced a tremendous understanding of observation of behaviour, of analysis of behaviour, and of doing something constructive and creative as an answer to human needs.

The teacher constantly reevaluates the projects and events the children are involved in in terms of the child rather than the other way around; she realizes that as the child grows and synthesizes material there will be many plateaus, many pauses, some going back to simpler concepts on the climb to more complex activity. The child who is safe in his knowledge of his acceptability to the teacher feels free to return to simpler activities, to refresh himself, and then to begin the arduous climb up the next hill. The teacher recognizes that there will be hills and valleys and plains and perhaps some unconquerable mountains in each child's path and is handy with encouragement and guidance for the child's self-identity. She realizes that the child's self-picture which is developing out of his relationship with her and out of his explorations of his world is a fragile thing. It needs nourishment, not overfeeding; protection, not dominance,᾿ stimulation, but not overpowering awesomeness. The child whose self-picture is healthy sees himself as an exploring and curious person and one who is not too afraid — and he will learn. If he cannot view himself this way, then he does not learn; he may memorize, but he does not acquire skills which will enable him to go from one subject matter to another.

This teacher is an "interactionist" who must not only be constantly aware of the developing children she is working with but also think about the organization and structure of the classroom, about timetabling, about materials and their complexity. Not all teachers can work this way. Some are information-givers and should not be forced to be otherwise. These teachers have real value if they are brought into the classroom by the interactionist teacher as resource persons. The resource teacher has no influence on structure but does have special knowledge to impart. It is up to the interactionist teacher and the child to then make use of the information, and to make use of it in ways which are most suitable to the child.[6]

The Teacher and His Relationship with His Peers

Along with the traditional form of subject content and evaluation, other rigidities of the outdated educational system need to be abandoned. The teachers in this new system need to discuss and question with an open attitude; they need to relate to each other as people, not just as teachers of particular subjects whose closed classrooms are their own little kingdoms, inviolate to criticism except from above by the occasional wandering supervisor or administrator. They have to freely express opinions and ideas among themselves or this method will not work. Because the teaching methods are very visible, they are very open to criticism. When you have this kind of high visibility factor and you do not have the ordinary pedagogical hierarchical system operating, then new questions can be asked: Is the student motivated? Cooperative? Withdrawn? What is his personality? What is the relationship between student and teacher? What kind of questions will help him to evolve a project? Are there other ways I may approach material so as to interest him? We must remember that these questions arise out of an ideology of education in danger of evolving into a crushing monster which could halt this openness, for it is housed in a society which demands information, a state of knowledge rather than ways of knowing. Therefore there must be continuous questioning between teacher and student, so that each keeps the other focussed through feedback on their common goal. This is not the current institution-based feedback method which places value judgments on what *should* be remembered or learned. Rather it asks what *have* you understood, what are you going to look at, how are you going to look at this, what do you need, what can I help you with? There is no limitation, no "knowledge is now ended, you can forget all you have learned and begin on another subject, you know all you need to know or all the semester allows time for." Implicit in this new method is the idea that knowledge is never ending and the feeling that each child has the potential to keep on learning and growing with the world around him.

I am presenting a more difficult way of teaching, for I am asking the teacher to have a knowledge of what the child is able to do at a certain age, how to approach him so that he is involved and concerned about the task presented, and how to help him integrate the ideas he has with the teacher's, so that he grows. I am suggesting, as I have throughout this book, that play is the medium through which learning proceeds, and that is different from saying that learning proceeds in a structured environment. I am saying that it is the unstructured environment, one which recognizes the child's uniqueness, his self-confidence, and his abilities and then presents materials to him with guidelines and safety, which allows effective learning and teaching to go on. This is a challenge because security of structure, of rights and wrongs, of "I have all the answers" is changed to one where the teacher observes the child and, using knowledge of human development, helps the child to acquire information and skills through the medium which is most available to the child: play.

CHAPTER 6

THE ENVIRONMENT:
CLASSROOM — COMMUNITY — HOME

JUST as I have pointed out that a school's curriculum cannot be made up of isolated subjects and create a successful learning environment, so I must point out that the school experience of the child cannot be isolated from his home and community experience. By the same token the teacher, in the progression of the child's growing awareness, cannot be a person separate and apart from other persons who people his world. People, events, and environments are an integrated reality of the child.

We all know that education does not occur in a vacuum; the established system does pay lip service to the idea of beginning with the child's origins and taking his individual personality and background into account. But I do not feel that it *really* recognizes the extent to which the young child first entering the school is a product of his own very special world. Let us look at what he brings with him into his first classroom.

First, each child will arrive in that classroom with a bundle of ideas which not only stem from his parents and his immediate family's attitudes, but also from the feelings, attitudes, and ideas of his neighbourhood. He has begun to explore the fields surrounding his house or the gutter at his doorstep, and he has found in these various places many objects and ideas which fascinate him and lead him into further exploration, both physical and mental. Certain objects and materials will be familiar and comfortable to him, and he needs to find these in his classroom too, so that it becomes a transition area from the home and neighbourhood into the school.

In the years he has spent at home with his family, the child has formed a picture of himself in relation to other people: as a son or daughter, a brother or sister, niece or nephew, or grandchild. He has some ideas about what is appropriate and acceptable to adults who stand in various roles to him, and it will take some time before the child finds out these things about this new dimension, the classroom and the teacher. The teacher, if she observes carefully, will find out a good deal about the authority, style, and expectations which are familiar to the child and with which he may initially be most comfortable.

The child arriving at school for the first time has been learning since the moment he could hear and see and feel and taste. He has a clearly developed cognitive style which allows him to look at situations in particular ways, and to approach new ideas or objects in a distinctive manner; this again is largely a product of the ways in which he was encouraged to experience and explore his home environment, the ways in which adults have structured his world and communicated with him about it. It is important that the teacher recognize the learning style which the child already has, and then provide the child with the opportunity to grow from that place, in an environment where he will feel at home, which provides both old and new materials, and encourages exploration, curiosity, and questioning.

There is a wide variance in the abilities, skills, learning styles, needs, and personality characteristics evident in children when they come to school, and it is interesting to speculate on the causes for these variations. Partly they are a result of heredity; certainly no behavioural pattern or characteristic can develop without an underlying basis of genetic potentiality. In an environment which is beneficial and satisfying to the child, the genetic endowment blossoms most fully. The less favourable the environment, the less opportunity the genetic capacities of the child have for full development.[26] Thus, the child who has grown up with a dietary deficiency must surely show this effect in his later behaviour.[19] Perhaps a more meaningful example might be one where the child has a very poor diet, or even lacks food, and as a result responds most often either with aggression or feelings of fatigue. This child has very little opportunity to partake of the environmental array of stimulation because he is too busy defending himself against what seems to him noxious stimuli, because he is hungry and tired. Such a child would certainly not be able to learn in the classroom and might need to be fed by the teacher before any learning could actually proceed. To ask for learning in such circumstances is to invite aggression; and it therefore becomes very important for the teacher to recognize, and be very sensitive to, the needs of such a child and to be prepared to satisfy these needs in order for learning to proceed.

There is another very special problem one finds in large cities with vigorous immigration activity. It is perhaps impossible for anyone who has not gone through it to recognize what a shock school must be at first for children whose family patterns or cultural background has ill-prepared them for existing in the English-speaking school systems. Most of us moved easily to school from homes where we were gradually prepared for school: we learned colours, numbers, time concepts, and vocabularies for homes, stores, playgrounds, trips, weather, the seasons — in our family language. Kindergarten was simply an extension of all those words and the ideas for which they stood. The child whose background has included all these ideas in another language is forced to accommodate himself with great speed and under real pressure to the reality of the "English classroom."[36] We will see the results of that struggle for years; for many non-English-speaking children, it has equalled failure in school in the early years, especially in learning to read, and has resulted in streaming and perhaps in their eventual early school leaving. This is certainly a major problem with which the schools have failed to deal adequately. In Toronto a recent report to the school board indicated the desirability of beginning children's schooling in their first language and gradually introducing English over the first three or four years as the language of instruction. Obviously this will be a costly and difficult plan to implement, but just as obviously it is necessary if the real waste of human potential which currently occurs is to be stopped.

Individual variations in responsivity and sensitivity to the classroom environment and to the teacher are a result not only of general interaction between genotype and environment, but also of the relationship and interaction between parents and child.[27] Not only do the parents influence the child, but the child influences the parents and know it; this interaction marches into the classroom with him on the first day.[24] Thus, not only does the teacher influence the child but vice versa. Every teacher has had a child with whom he or she had considerable difficulty working, who really evoked negative reactions and made him feel guilty as adult and professional. It is important to recognize that this is an inevitable part of reactions between two individual human beings and to take steps to counter it, because otherwise the child, in turn, responds either by growing aggression and hostility or by absenteeism and apathy. Then he is well on the way to failure. The teacher must be aware enough of this kind of individual variation and reaction to try to involve the child positively in classroom activities. It takes a skillful teacher to recognize the effects a child has on her and to try to understand these to the point where her ability to work with the child is not destroyed or negatively influenced. Occasionally a child will simply be impossible for the teacher to work with in a healthy way. It must be realized that this is not evidence of lack of teaching ability or proof of a personality flaw, but simply an unfortunate fact which dictates open and frank discussion with the principal about alternate placement of the child, to be done in such a way that neither the child nor the family sees it as punishment or as a condemnation or rejection of the child as a person. This is obviously a last attempt, a difficult and painful process, but one which is essential to the emotional and psychological well-being of both child and teacher.[11]

The child brings many things to school with him: his experiences as part of a family and a neighbourhood, a cultural identity and language patterns, a distinctive cognitive style, and a wide variance in abilities, skills, and personality characteristics. All of these have contributed to, and make up part of, his self-image, his identity as an individual human being. He has gradually come to perceive himself in ways which say "I am all right, I am succeeding, I am liked" — or the opposites of these attitudes. The major determinants of a child's self-image seem to be the way he was provided with stimulation, given adult warmth and comfort, and the degree of gratification or frustration in his family circle. I believe it is the responsibility of those involved in the educational system to understand the particular child-rearing attitudes in a family so that they may add to these in a meaningful way for the child rather than create distress, distrust, and disillusionment. Children need to have the feeling of love and acceptance and affection and approval from their parents as an ongoing part of their lives. If the learning environment set up in the classroom creates anxiety about these basic needs, then learning cannot proceed effectively. The child's identity is intrinsically bound up with the satisfactions he receives from his home, and teachers must be sensitive to each child's sense of identity and respect his heritage.

Although I seem to have set a tremendous task here for educators, it is not so awesome if we consider the naturalness of learning through play and self-discovery. The child will, in so many ways, teach the teacher about himself. If the basic groundwork of respect for many ways of life has been laid down, teacher and child can come to a mutual agreement to learn from each other; the child will accept the teacher as his guide and will open yet more aspects of himself to her.

These are some of the things which children bring to school with them. Now what are some of the things which teachers have to bring to school with them? I have touched on many of them already: sensitivity to individual variations and needs, knowledge about different family child-rearing practices and cultural backgrounds, flexibility in providing experiences and materials, warmth and acceptance of a child as a total person, honesty with children, parents, each other, and principals. Many practical skills are also essential for the teacher of young children. I believe a knowledge of child developmental theory, of psychological growth, and of what constitutes sound learning experiences for young children are also essential.

As well as sound factual information about learning theories, teachers of the young must have a thorough understanding of the complexities of the dependency relationships between young children and their parents, particularly their mothers, if they are to cushion the child's initial adjustment to school and facilitate his continued sound psychological growth. The relationship of the mother and the child is the most important and vital factor in the child's development, with influence upon his physical development, his intellectual achievement, and his psychological growth. For example, very early continued separation of the mother from the infant seems to result in the "wasting away" of the infant physically (Spitz).[39] Early rejection of the child seems to result in an overly independent and, at times, antisocial child (Stern, Weininger).[40,43] Over protectiveness seems to result in an anxious child who wants to please and is fearful of expressing any kind of aggression (Pinkus, Spitz, Stern, Weininger).[34,39,41,43] That these attitudes have an effect on learning is well documented,[28] and children who have been reared in such atmospheres seem to be destined to require special help.[11] Where the child is not provided with sufficient individual stimulation and encouragement, either because there is a weak attachment between mother and infant or because this familial atmosphere is such that the child is not encouraged to explore, to learn, to talk with his mother, then the child is deprived and will require encouragement in the classroom to explore and learn.

It is important for teachers to recognize that dependency relationships are the kind with which young children feel safest, with which they are most familiar. A certain amount of transference of the child's relationship with his mother to his first teacher is thus almost inevitable; not only does the child know best how to relate in that way, but it fills his needs for continuity, security, and predictability until he finds his feet in this new environment. Thus, it is very important for the classroom teacher to be the kind of person who feels comfortable about touching and holding young children, about providing warmth and care. This is true not only in the lower grades, but all the way through the junior high school years — the one way to guarantee safety and acceptance to children of all ages is by our willingness to extend ourselves physically as well as verbally to them. Children know something we often forget: it seems quite possible to lie to someone with words, almost impossible to do so with touch. Mutual respect and trust are expressed by the gentle touch of one person to another. Our schools would be richer if we could remember that it is trust which underlies our learning experiences from the day we take our first step, secure in the knowledge that mother is there to catch us if we fall.

Another basic part of the dependency relationship of child to mother, child to teacher, is the need for acceptance. A child needs to be certain that even if you as an adult reject his behaviour in no uncertain terms, you accept him as a person — he is not stupid or dumb or crazy or careless in your eyes just because a particular piece of his behaviour is one of those things. Every action, every word, every touch needs to transmit the feeling to the child that "Even if I do not like what you just did and will not allow you to do it again, I like *you*. *You* are *not* this bit of your behaviour — it is only a part of your way of dealing with people, which you can alter and change as you go on."

Trust and acceptance of the child as a valuable person, coupled with the ability to let the child determine his own needs for dependence and independence, are the basis for a viable and satisfying relationship between child and teacher. The teacher is not in competition with the child's mother or family but rather is a continuation of the security which they provide, a bridge to a frightening but exciting world. The child needs to be able to maintain a relatedness to his family and his environment. The teacher must recognize this need and not alienate a child from his family but help to integrate the new classroom experiences in such a way that the child participates rather than withdraws, feels safe and comfortable rather than left out and afraid, and has a sense of joy, a sense of fulfillment and promise, rather than a sense of doom and alienation.

CHAPTER 7

THE GROWING SELF — ARRESTED

THE average educated North American usually thinks of the "deprived" child as coming from a vaguely identifiable strata of society labelled lower class or working class somehow denoting an economically distressed group of people. There is some truth in this; there is a correlation between economic deprivation and the deprived child; to try to state otherwise is to be ideologically naive. Another euphemism is the "culturally disadvantaged," which does not sound quite so debilitating.

When I speak of a "deprived" child, I mean a child who is deprived emotionally, physically, and intellectually, who has a cultural disadvantage in regard to his peers who have come from an environment rich in warmth and in cognitive stimuli through encouragment in play and energetic exploration. These children can be found everywhere and include the mildly disoriented as well as the severely disturbed.[51] I do know that deprived children are children who distort their world, who are unable to redefine their comprehensive maps in regard to reality. When this happens, the distortion becomes cumulative. Then the child operates on the basis that it is not so much that I am looking at things wrongly, but that other people are attacking me and preventing me from doing what I want to do." The projections of such a child seem to be the consequence of lack of satisfaction and inability to alter the fantasy distortions of the comprehensive map.

Teachers of these young people have discovered that culturally disadvantaged children who were not given much opportunity to play and experiment within their home environment come to school with a different linguistic, perceptual, and cognitive repertory than the child who has had a rich play life.[2] The child may not communicate as much; he may not look at toys and play materials as things to be manipulated.[3] He is accustomed to less language in his home, and often is a child who has been told "Don't touch — you'll break it." His natural drive to touch and to understand his world has been smothered by his environment. He has learned that in his home he must behave in a certain way. To do otherwise is to risk rejection, hurt, or deprivation. When this young child comes to school, there is no reason why he should not think that the teacher, another adult, is going to behave in the same way as have other adults in his life. The child is then restricted in what he may do and really has to be helped to play and to explore. It is as though the teacher must give the child permission to play. She must create the kind of sufficiently safe environment for the child so that he may risk altering his prior understanding that to play is dangerous. The teacher certainly cannot say "Go and play." This is rather meaningless to the child, who already knows that he can not. The teacher must help the child bridge this gap by providing home-like materials, by using the materials herself, by becoming involved with the play herself, and by inviting the child to "Come and do things with me." She must encourage him to talk in whatever way is available to him: If the child talks in phrases without verbs, if the words are always in the imperative, or if the child asks single word questions, then the child should not only be allowed but encouraged to use his or her form of language. The teacher answers in her language, but does not attempt to either complicate her speech form or to correct the child's speech. It is by imitation, modelling, identification, and involvement with the relationship provided by the teacher that the child's language and communication patterns will change. If change is demanded, then learning appears to be slowed down and the opportunity for creative play with language becomes lessened.

As I said earlier, there are varying degrees of disturbed children. If the child cannot function at all, he is officially labelled severely disturbed and is moved from the mainstream of the educational system into a specialized education, perhaps in the form of a treatment centre or special school. Most of my professional life has been involved with these children and what I have learned from them has motivated me to search for a better educational system for all children.

I have emphasized the importance of removing whatever may seem foreign from the classroom. For the severely disturbed child this is absolutely imperative. When he enters the classroom he must begin at a point which is familiar and safe for him. The teacher needs to be sufficiently sensitive to, and understanding of, the emotional needs of the child so as not to simply provide equipment or books because they seem age-appropriate but to recognize that the child's emotional life will determine the selection and use of materials. For example, when we have a twelve-year-old who is emotionally and socially deprived with a long history of academic problems, it would be worthless to force him into a specific academic remedial reading program. It would be wiser to provide him with materials in a classroom which meet his early emotional and social needs. The teacher recognizes where and how the child can start to learn the academic material which our society wants him to learn. For example, the teacher helps the child through the formidable process of changing child-play with numbers to arithmetical functioning at an appropriate level. Under the guidance and leadership of this teacher the child will learn, but only if the teacher is aware of the very early needs of this child which have prevented him from learning thus far in school.

The disturbed child entering a regular school finds that his familiar reactions are inadequate to cope with the frustrating world of the average classroom, and his decreased ability to deal with this results in behaviour which is unacceptable in the classroom. Fighting, withdrawal, swearing, autistic thinking, and depression are some of the consequences of this inability to deal with the classroom world.

For the disturbed child I am suggesting that the usual stages of learning (the active stage, the pictorial stage, the symbolic stage)[9] are not seen as separate but rather as interwoven and useful for the child at any stage in his learning. Thus, I would expect the child to manipulate, to act upon materials in his environment, to communicate in gestures, to look at or handle things for a long period of time, to use all his senses. All these kinds of activities, usually thought of as being in the active stage of learning, should also involve the pictorial stage, where the child is provided with the opportunity to look for similarities, to have models of activities such as toys and small representations of his environment like houses and trees, and the teacher is provided with opportunities to watch him as he matches, sorts, classifies, and orders. This pictorial stage intermingles with the active stage in such a way that the teacher will see that at times language is complex and judgments are accurate; at other times language is simple, illogical, and not connected with the activity as might be anticipated in the active stage. If the teacher provides the opportunity for the child to talk about his experience, to record his experience, to talk about the patterns, and to ask for explanations, then he is making use of what has been termed the symbolic stage of learning.

To do this the child must have enough time to do all his work, to use materials and situations in such a way that he can explore and replay new and old possibilities. We encourage the child to make his own interpretations and to do so with the teacher as a guide rather than as an authority or repository of right answers. In this way, the child begins to extend his competencies without his former fear of applying them to new situations and finding out they will not work. By the time he is ready to apply them to new situations, he has the flexibility to accept and synthesize whatever results, because the crippling fear of failure, so thoroughly inculcated by many of our public school systems, has been carefully and systematically neutralized.

The process of relating the academic achievement to the child's emotional needs is a psychoeducational one which encourages the child to depend upon the teacher as a person who is a guiding, resourceful catalyst. In this way, the primitive components of the child's ego-functioning are supported by the relationship, and use of these components is facilitated. Gradually, as the ego functions (such as motor skills, retention, judgment, and comprehension) develop, the child is given the opportunity through the classroom environment to master specific competencies which he has either not approached before or viewed only as difficult, if not impossible, tasks. This psychoeducational process is dependent on providing the child with interpersonal involvement, with dependency satisfaction, classroom stimulation, reality orientation, and repetition through play of experiences and tasks which previously had been frightening for the child. In this environment the child can practise, repeat, and explore skills and competencies, can manoeuvre and manipulate his environment in ways which provide for creativity and which contribute to the next growing phase of his psychological development and to his capacity to obtain and integrate academic information.

What about the disturbed child who remains in the public school system? Perhaps the school is in a poor area of the city and we encounter the problem of the lower class child, economically and culturally deprived.

The first problem of the school in coping with these children is that the teachers are rarely prepared to provide the lower class child with what he can handle and needs, and they are seldom able to overcome their own middle-class backgrounds long enough to be nonjudgmental and accepting of standards at wide variance with their own. It is a kind of mental nose-turning-up which the overly sensitive antennae of the children pick up at once, and despise and fear.

The rigidity of many teachers when faced by superficialities (such as vulgarities or obscenities, dirty faces and hands, body odours untouched by soap or deodorant) puts a gulf ten miles wide between them and their students, a gap neither will try to cross in the ten months they must endure each other. Because the teacher cannot understand that words, promises, threats, and bribes mean little or nothing, and because often she cannot bring herself to touch or smile or caress (as I said, touch doesn't lie, which the children know instinctively and the teacher senses vaguely) or come out from behind her role as the power, the grown-up, very little that is real happens in many classrooms. The teacher says what teachers from time immemorial have said about cleanliness and honesty and neatness and punctuality and the children do not hear a word. What they hear is the vibration of distrust, of uncaring, of not wanting to know what their lives are like outside the classroom because it might make one's middle-class comfort slightly less comfortable on a scale which can not be altered by giving to the United Appeal antiseptically. These children react as the intelligent, sensitive human beings they are by retreating to a place where this person, this teacher, will never reach them. They do not want to be treated as *things* — that has been the story of their lives, and of their parents' lives. It is safer to be compliant at a distance, to tune out, to resign themselves to the ignorance and prejudice of the authorities around them, than to assert themselves futilely. The children in these teachers' hands have not found that acting like a person has many socially redeeming values, and the teacher's sense of unease and inability to interact on a personal, human level with them only confirms this reality once again.

Most teachers are acutely aware of the deficiencies of the schools in terms of education methodology and curriculum: the restlessness, boredom, acting out behaviour, and total lack of success in terms of either testable results or a personal "feeling" of understanding on the part of the students are things they know only too well on a day-to-day, firing-line basis. It occasionally occurs to me that these students and teachers have more in common than they realize in terms of the way they experience the classroom, as quiet desperation mixed with utter boredom. Teachers *know* that what they are teaching and how it is being taught are often totally irrelevant to the lives of their students; students *sense* that what they are learning is meaningless — but both sides keep up some pretense, going on with the old game. If you admit that what you are doing is practically worthless, how can you endure it for another day, much less the rest of the year? And how do you justify the enormous sums of public money, your own long years in university, your choosing of this as your life's work, if it does not matter after all? Most teachers, especially in inner city "problem" schools, would grasp only too eagerly at any ideas which would salvage something from the chaos in the classroom — not only to save the children, but to save their own self-respect, to feel like professionals again.

Dog-eared copies of *How Children Fail,*[21] *Schools Without Failure,*[18] *The Naked Children,*[15] and *Teaching as a Subversive Activity,*[35] read avidly, agreed with vehemently, and put down with a sigh, are mute evidence of the dissatisfaction of many teachers with the schools, the curriculum, the methods and the nonlearning all around them.

SECTION II

INTRODUCTION

As I mentioned earlier, during the past years I have been involved in the assessment and diagnosis of children labelled disturbed, and in the implementation of the social and clinical programs designed for them. These children need a great deal of help.

The children I have seen were referred by various community agencies such as Children's Aid Societies, Family Service Associations, the Juvenile Courts, Boards of Education, treatment centres; from private sources such as lawyers, physicians, psychiatrists, and, increasingly, from parents themselves. I personally have found it very gratifying to see that parents have become sufficiently involved and understanding of their children's problems to intervene themselves as early as possible.

Many times, the problems referred to me have been things like inability to work in school. At times, this inability to work has been labelled with the diagnosis of a learning disability and, sometimes more precisely, a visual-motor handicapped child or a child suffering from psychomotor problems. However, this kind of seeming differentiation from the general to the specific has been a misdiagnosis, and the preciseness has only lent considerable confusion to the field. This kind of diagnosis really lets the school, parent, and society off the hook: If it is a neurological problem, then certainly neither the school nor the parent can be to blame, and the child's failure is not so painful to the adults around him! In addition, children have been referred to us because they are hyperactive, delinquent, socially immature, or have social adjustment problems. Some are said to be incorrigible or unteachable; some are labelled brain-damaged or mentally retarded. At times, children have been sent to us with the diagnosis of psychoneurosis, and it is only with considerable trepidation that we unlock Pandora's box to find out what, in fact, is meant by psychoneurosis. These problems are multidimensional (as well as reflecting the semantic confusion prevalent in educational psychology today). However, one thing is always clear — the child has suffered, is suffering, and (unless we do something about it) will continue to suffer both as a child and as an adult.

The following dialogues were a sharing of information between a resource teacher involved in developing a method of teaching the unteachable and myself. It was a process of discovery for both of us, not without its setbacks and quandaries, but behind the reality of every word we spoke were the children in need of building for themselves a person they could respect and in whom they could take pleasure.

Adam's function in this process was not as a trained psychologist (for he was not one) but more than the conventional idea of a teacher. His role is much like the one mentioned in Section I, only more so, for in working with disturbed children the intensity and time involvement principle is more concentrated. Play was the basis upon which we progressed and the success of this progress was greatly dependent upon Adam's willingness and ability to give freedom and license to play in the classroom, or the "room" as it came to be known. With play as our foundation, we worked toward the development of a project or projects for each child, as a method of providing a bridge for the child between his old frustrations and sense of limitations to new capabilities and hence an enlightened, enlarged sense of the child's potential both as a rational and emotional individual. With each child we also introduced the concept of their "book or books" — a binder(s) which contained work they had done, things they had found, anything the children considered important to them. It was their personal chronicle of achievement and self-knowledge and as such, served as a building block of self-esteem. These binders were extremely important to our program.

In this case, with these children, there was a deliberate attempt to create a relationship between Adam and each child.

No amount of theorizing will ever supplant the visible, practical evidence of a child coming into his own. All the children mentioned in these dialogues "made it" and emerged as healthy individuals, not in control of their lives but in charge.

I will give you a brief summary of their backgrounds, who they were before they reached us.

Peter

Peter was a very attractive, blond-haired little boy, somewhat untidy, occasionally with a dirty face, affectionate to everyone, friendly to strangers, and made friends easily.

He was first referred to us as a child completely out of control, in court for setting seven fires. This had been happening for some time and was, indeed, a very serious charge. He came from a broken home, on a low socioeconomic level, and only saw his father occasionally. He had two younger sisters and had recently set fire to the bed of one of them. He was also charged with breaking and entering a number of summer cottages, pouring gasoline in one of them and setting it on fire. He stole things, fought, and was destructive, and was very defiant and stubborn towards authority figures.

He had difficulty telling reality from fantasy. He was unable to talk about his feelings, was hyperactive, and had some difficulty in pronouncing *r* and *l,* though he was fluent in the rest of his speech. For quite some time after he came to us, it was difficult to keep Peter safe from harm because he just did not seem to see dangers; it was thought that his frequent inability to distinguish what was real from what was not was the cause of this. He liked physical activities such as tobogganing and wrestling. Peter liked to be hugged and cuddled. He was six years old when he came to us.

Lily

A pretty girl, Lily came from a family with many, many problems and a very chaotic and unhappy history. The father and mother, both of whom were very promiscuous, separated and rejoined many times. The father left home for the last time about a year and a half before Lily came to us. Neither parent seemed able to give much affection to the children. The mother seemed to treat Lily with greater severity than she did the other two children, and Lily as a child was seen as a "sour-puss," rarely happy or contented, moody, a chronic complainer, fighting with everyone, having no friends, and becoming more difficult to discipline. She was usually poorly dressed, certainly not at all warmly enough in the winter, with no gloves, socks instead of long stockings or tights. The children were close and protective of one another for a time, then became mutually jealous. The mother said there was a barrier between herself and Lily; they just could not seem to be close to one another.

Lily seemed to want to model herself on her mother: at times the mother was dry-eyed through trouble and sometimes she wept. Lily kept pace with her. The mother was often seductive with new friends and Lily tried to be the same. Apparently there was some strange relationship between Lily and an old man living "downstairs" until she was seven and mentioned it to her mother. Lily never talked about this.

In the first months of her stay with us she was very insecure, seeking constant attention and approval from both teachers and other students. She would try to present a good facade but would tease and anger others when no one was watching. She was ten years old when she first came to us.

Rachel

Rachel was not quite ten when she arrived, a plump, dark-haired and dark-eyed little girl with freckles and a wide grin.

Her mother had a long history of emotional problems, requiring hospitalization at various times. An older brother was already in treatment for severe problems. Rachel clung to her mother to an unusual extent, had frequent nightmares, fought with the children at school, and had many temper tantrums. Her mother brought her in for treatment reluctantly. Rachel had a voracious appetite when she was nervous and upset. The difficult relationship between mother and child was considered to be the base of Rachel's problems. Although the mother said she "could not exist without Rachel," she realized that treatment was essential, otherwise Rachel's problems were bound to increase and become more and more severe. The mother took her out of treatment three times because she wanted her back so badly.

Rachel was afraid of rejection, of being cut off from the caring of the giving person if she showed hostility and anger. She was hyperactive, impulsive, and needed a positive, secure, trusting relationship with a female. She was constantly anxious and became very disorganized, and many quite ordinary things in daily life frightened her.

Anne

A teenager when she came to us (17) she was a slim, rather small girl, who seemed young for her age.

She was the daughter of a concert pianist and an adoring overprotective father who died when Anne was eight. She developed heart trouble at six months of age and had heart surgery when she was eight. This was successful, although considerable care of her health had to be taken for quite some time. Until about twelve years old, she appeared as "sweet, dreamy, rather autistic looking." Her mother remarried when she was ill and Anne was always hostile to the new husband. She had never made many friends and now became withdrawn and sullen, increasingly antagonistic toward her mother. She then drifted into a group of alienated and antisocial youth, was used sexually, and introduced to drugs. When she was fifteen, she became pregnant but aborted spontaneously. She does not seem to have participated actively in all of this, but passively, more drifting with the tide.

CHAPTER 8

DIALOGUES

THIS was not our first session together, but it was early in our experiment with this kind of teaching program. Adam had been working with Peter and Lily and was just beginning to build a relationship with them. We had been discussing "the room" Adam was creating, the importance of book shelves within easy reach of the children, arranged so the books could be picked up and discarded at will; the idea of availability of books, but not in such a way as to overwhelm a child with too many choices; to avoid a confusing atmosphere in favour of an environment which made sense to the children.

Adam was very concerned about how the room would work, but he realized that the essential thing was that the room "grew" as his relationship with the children "grew."

Adam: Many people have already noticed the room has changed.

Dr. Otto: Now I am suggesting your tentacles go out further than just your room.

Adam: I feel they haven't — well, Peter has extended a little by taking books.

Dr. Otto: Yes, he has. And you'll find that more of the kids will do this very naturally and easily. When Peter says "Let's go into your room," you know the boy doesn't have to go into that room every time he sees you, but he's going in to play and have fun. Playing with toys is a very legitimate thing and is a contribution to this child's education. But we don't want him to feel, every time he sees you, that you are connected with a kind of work, when the kind of work we're really trying to evolve for this child is play.

Adam: By the way, when I brought the bricks in for the shelves, Peter was there and was kind of loose and interested in helping make the shelves, so he pounded away for over an hour with a cold chisel; they were old fire bricks with cement on them, and he worked on them for a long time with me.

Dr. Otto: Well, that would be very good. He's showing you he's sufficiently interested in what you are doing together to work for an hour on those old bricks — I mean, it's an important room. He's telling you how important it is by offering his services to the construction of that room. How's he doing, by the way? How's his book coming?

Adam: He hasn't done much. He did go away and try to play with it. He took another folder and put some pictures on the front, but it fell apart. Then he couldn't get it back into the holes again and that was one of the problems, and I said I would fix his book for him. So his book is fixed and he'll see that it's fixed.

Dr. Otto: How do you see it progressing, in terms of how he is using the book? Do you think that it's at a standstill at this point?

Adam: Well, he put in this very, very important greeting card from some relative and I suppose that makes it pretty important. . . The way I see Peter using the books is that he has to have a whole bunch of books.

Dr. Otto: What do you mean, a whole bunch of books?

Adam: One book has the stories in it, another book has some little pictures in it that he cut out of some magazine, and this one has the card in it. He never puts them all together.

Dr. Otto: But he may.

Adam: He may, yes. But at this point it seems to me he wants to make a variety of them. He hasn't made any more, just the three.

Dr. Otto: Fine. I wouldn't push him for more variety, but I would help him to make use of these three books. Also, help him to talk about the significance of the card and how one book is especially devoted to the card. He may want to tell you about the card. If he wishes to make a story about this and wants it in one of the three books, then I'd help him to do that. I would return periodically to these books and help him either to talk about them or put something into them by suggesting this is a pretty important thing that he's done, would he like to put it in one of the books? And which book would he like to put it in?

Adam: I've been doing that. We went to the library this week —

Dr. Otto: Good. Going to the library is very important for Peter; here you've done something that he's not done before.

Adam: He asked the librarian for the dinosaur book. No, first of all he had to get his card renewed because he'd lost his first one. Anyway, the librarian showed him where there were a number of dinosaur books.

Dr. Otto: Was he overwhelmed by this?

Adam: There were two rows.

Dr. Otto: Too much.

Adam: So he pulled some out, the biggest ones, but he could only take four. He took the four he wanted and I took one out as well on my card, and he wanted to know what it was. I told him it was a dinosaur book, that I was interested in it, too. Anyway, it really was interesting, the librarian asked him to write his library card number on the cards in the back of the books. his number was 46368 — he writes the 3 backwards, which she didn't seem to mind. He got to the last book and the number of the last person who had used it was 46369! He was very excited about that.

Dr. Otto: He recognized that!

Adam: Yes, he did. So quite a bit was happening there.

Dr. Otto: Obviously a lot happened in what looked like incidental things.

Adam: Exactly, that's what I'm starting to notice.

Dr. Otto: So what you really want to do is try to set up the environment so that the incidental things, which may not be so incidental in our thinking, are happening. Going to the library is not so incidental; it was planned on the basis of trying to study further something that you had already started in school, so it made sense to Peter and to you, and going to the library permitted you to do a number of other things, like writing, selecting, sorting, discussing, relating to the librarian.

Adam: There were some pictures on the wall; I wanted to see them and he came along. I was trying to say, well, it looks as though these are very ancient, from a very old book. They were drawings; some rich man had been trying to make the nicest prayer book possible. The librarian came in and started telling too much. Peter lost interest, though he listened to her for some time because she was so nice. I said to her "You have given Peter an awful lot of interesting things, but we have to go now." She could tell she had overdone it.

Dr. Otto: Maybe she learned something as a result of all that, too.

Adam: Peter might be asking to go to the library a lot now —

Dr. Otto: Good, but do try to make it relevant in terms of something he is interested in, not just something that you are interested in or something that at the moment you assume to be of value for the child to see. Don't just take him to a tanning factory out of the blue.

Adam: I know. He said "I want to go someplace," and I said, "There are all kinds of places we can go — where do you want to go?"

Dr. Otto: He can't answer that.

Adam: No.

We talked further about Peter who had the beginnings of a project without realizing it, and we could help him to extend it. A visit to the Royal Ontario Museum in Toronto to see their dinosaur collection would make sense. He could do drawings of what he saw, plastercasts, write about it if he wished. Adam would guide him from an understanding of what kind of thinking arrangements Peter had about his world now, what

Peter's motivation was to do things.

Dr. Otto: Peter started off at a pretty low level, but now you have him with three books, you have him dealing with those books, putting something into them. You've already gone to the library, you have sorted out things there; he was interested in snakes, and now you've moved from snakes to dinosaurs.

Adam: He has contributed to the room.

Dr. Otto: He's contributed to the room. You have the possibility now of extending this dinosaur and snake project by making things.

Adam: He's used people other than myself to help him learn what he wants to know.

Dr. Otto: Right, and he is learning

Adam: He would be very interested in going to the museum — in going to Toronto. I know, because he's suggested that. I'm trying to think about where he's at now and where he has been. When he's on his own in the school he doesn't seem to be able to do much. And there are quite a few children like that who have the staff very frustrated.

Dr. Otto: But you see, the children are being asked to dream up projects, they're being asked what they want to do and they can't answer that. That's why we're trying to teach in a different way. You are the catalyst, the one who sets the environment; you motivate the child into discovering what he wants to do.

Adam: I seem to be doing that naturally — for instance, there was choir practice going on while Tommy was in the room. I actually saw him keeping time and I encouraged the person behind him to help. And then everybody got mad at Tommy because suddenly he was stomping about the room. I explained to them he was marching. Then Tommy marched up to the stage, and one of the kids got really mad at him, but I said it shouldn't interfere with their singing to have him up on the stage. Someone suggested that maybe he could march on the floor instead, but he really wanted to be up on the stage marching. So, this sort of thing I get into as well.

Dr. Otto: Well, I suppose it's hard to understand how important it is for Tommy to be able to keep time, and that keeping time is extremely important if he is going to do a number of other things which we hope he's going to develop.

Adam: For all kinds of coordination. I'll tell you, everyone was pretty interested in his marching!

Dr. Otto: I'm sure. Okay, then, Peter's all set, this makes sense with Peter?

Adam: Oh, yes.

Dr. Otto: Now, there's a child you want to bring in to teach, who doesn't read now —

Adam: It's Allan.

Dr. Otto: Then I would suggest that you talk to Allan again and see if he would like to come.

Adam: Once a week only for him, too?

Dr. Otto: At first, if he can come once a week, and then afterwards, fine, if he can come more than once a week. That you'll have to arrange with him, it will have to be a mutual arrangement. The first meeting should be about exploring some of the things that he would like to learn from you in that environment through the relationship with you. Let him talk about that. Let him talk about whatever he wants to talk about. That doesn't necessarily mean that we are to start him on those things immediately. Tell him about the way in which we are going to try and work, not in such a way that it makes a very complicated sort of nonsense to him, but keep it very simple. As far as reading is concerned, try to find out what he knows. Don't pester him by giving him a formal test, but do ask him about things like knowing the letters of the alphabet and seeing whether he can actually write the alphabet. If he can't do those two things, then that's where we'll start. But don't do any of it in a formal, structured way which makes him feel like

"Ah, me! I'm in another testing situation." Do it in
an easy way.

Adam: Okay. Now I want to talk to you about Lily — I've
seen her for a while. I mentioned to you she likes to
get involved with shapes —

Dr. Otto: As far as Lily's concerned, use the shapes, use the
things she is bringing to you. Provide her with materials so that she can make more shapes, then see
whether or not it is difficult to make them. You may
find that it is very difficult, and then you can help
her.

Adam: You want *me* to see whether it is difficult to make
shapes?

Dr. Otto: Yes, for *you* to try to make squares, circles, cones,
diamonds, pyramids. If it is difficult for you, then it
is obviously going to be very difficult for her.

Adam: Oh, I see. Well, that's probably not too difficult for
me.

Dr. Otto: When you do it, you can see how it's done.

Adam: Oh, I see what you mean: so I go through it.

Dr. Otto: You see what's involved and then help her. You will
find that she may need paste or scotch tape, or you
may need masking tape.

Adam: We have all those things.

Dr. Otto: Fine. You'll need scissors, pencils, rules, too. From
there you will perhaps go on to the combining of
shapes. You know, what sort of things happen when
you put two triangles together. What we are eventually and gradually moving towards is a kind of arith-
metic, a kind of mathematics, a kind of geometry. I
think you could find out from the principal what the
curriculum is for grades 4 and 5, and then we can
discuss it and what sort of expectations we would
have, what sort of repetitions we can carry out with
Lily, and what sort of expectations she should have
for herself.

Adam: I wonder what kind of expectations she does have for
herself?

Dr. Otto: I think you'll find that out as you begin to talk about what she is doing, how she makes use of these shapes, what she would like to do with them. We can use shapes that she makes, we can use puzzles — certain kinds of puzzles, not an ordinary puzzle. I will try to get them for you.

Adam: She had some perfume bottles, she was doing some classifying.

Dr. Otto: She is classifying, but still — I'm not using the word "still" in a negative way — she's still incorporating, she's still trying to understand.

Adam: That's what I would say, too.

I left Adam with that — he would continue with Peter and Lily, and there was Allan coming up.

The following week we met again (this was to become a regular practise). Although the focus of Adam's work was centred around specific children, he was a curious being by nature and was always investigating situations and children apart from the "room."

Adam: Little things come up. I noticed, for instance, that people were cleaning up, but no sooner had they tossed stuff out than Jimmy would pick it up and save it. . . He likes to gather things, collect them.

Dr. Otto: Jimmy's a collector, then, and it's important that everybody realizes this and how it can be used. You can help the boy collect and it could very well be used as a school activity — help him to sort things, pile them, count them, write things. This sort of approach helps a child so he doesn't just feel like an oddball or a person who is there but not really willing to be there, or someone who just can't contribute anything.

Adam: Lily has been off shapes, you know. I think the reason was that it was "school work." We're working on three books with her — she thinks now that the book we started is going to be her picture book. She started writing down ideas and we started talking about them; we got into horses, somehow — that's something that she's very interested in. She even got a book from the library and I started her talking about them. She drew some diagrams, like this one. "This is a cart," she said.

Dr. Otto: A very simplified drawing of a cart.

Adam: She was struggling, I think, to draw a horse. I looked for some magazines. We found some pictures of horses; she cut them out, looked at them, and put them in her picture book. She went to the library alone: got a book on horses and we talked about them and she asked some questions. I encouraged her to write in her books, and we had a whole page on the things that she wanted to know.

Dr. Otto: How marvellous!

Adam: And she wrote the whole thing: three categories, and then we expanded them, and put points underneath, like headings. She said she would like to know more about horses. I asked where she might like to find out more about them and she said, "I might be able to get more books from the library." Then she added, "Maybe there'll be some things in the store." I said, "We might find somebody who has horses." "Yes!" she said, "We should go and see someone who has horses!"

Dr. Otto: You were really helping her, not telling her what to do, but helping her to keep the conversation open so she might lead it to the point where you both think she would be able to gain more information by going to see horses.

Adam: She went from trying to copy a horse to talking about horses; making a list of things she was interested in, while she also pursued it on her own, getting books, and now she's making plans for a visit. We had talked about it before, as a sort of problem, how to make it happen, and it was interesting that she picked it up so quickly. We had just come into the room when she said, "Yes, I would like to go."

"Oh, you mean about going to the farm?" "Yes," she said, "We have to find a place, find someone who is willing to tell us about it." David Blannet at the Red Wheel Farm has a horse and keeps it at Grant's. We went downstairs, she called Nancy at the office and got David Blannet's number and we tried to call him. He was out, but she wrote it down on her paper, his office number and his home number, and things she was going to ask him.

Dr. Otto: She was really organizing what she was doing.

Adam: She had everything written down. She had to leave and I said, "We'll call David and see if it's all right for us to make a visit."

Dr. Otto: That's great, I think that's just great! You brought her to the point where she could use the information that you were helping her to gain. She went from something that she had before, trying to draw a horse, which isn't really for her. Even though some people have suggested that she has enormous talent, actually she doesn't have this kind of talent. But now you're developing a project. You've made the visit possible, a hopeful thing, something that is meaningful in terms of this whole project. You're helping her to organize her thinking, to extend her thinking, to make use of whatever else is happening in her environment so that she's not dealing with just fantasy, she's pinning it into reality. This is really a development of herself.

Adam: She picked up the shapes again, just because they were in the drawer, I think. Oh, yes, there was the incident with the ruler. It was Lily's ruler and Peter was writing on it. I didn't want him to do that because it was Lily's and I just wanted to find a tactful way to redirect him.

Dr. Otto: What did you do?

Adam: I just said, "That's Lily's ruler and you really shouldn't write on it . . . buy you have written on it, so maybe we can rub it off." We did, a little. But he had been very anxious that whole day. I think what's bothering me is not that particular episode, but how to help Peter when he comes in a little high and not knowing what to do in the room. That day, he didn't want to do any more on his books, the books are "finished." He said, "I've had enough about snakes from the week before." I suggested we look into the books. He's very touchy about them. He has a very hard time entering anything.

Dr. Otto: You mean, he is almost sure that he is going to be criticized for what he does. Does he expect failure?

Adam: He has a fantasy about the book. He wants to put a lot of his Christmas cards into it. He already has a Christmas card from his relative in it, the one we talked about. I don't think he really has any other Christmas cards, but because that's what's on the first page he said, "That's going to be my Christmas card book." Somehow that seemed to go okay.

Dr. Otto: When Peter or any other child comes in, and he really looks anxious, and he is giving you enough clues that you realize he is pretty anxious and concerned, then you are not sure that he is going to do very much in terms of learning or in terms of participation that day. What I think you might want to try is going back to an activity that he has already accomplished, that was satisfying to him. In other words, help him to go back to something that was pleasurable, something he was able to do, which would help him to regain whatever it is that he has come to you for, that's preventing him from making use of the room. So it's like saying, "When you left me you were at point "c"; it looks like you're now at point "a." We're not going to criticize you for being at point "a" and we'll help you to regress, move backwards, in order to gain whatever stability you were beginning to feel at point "a" so that you can move on to point "c." That movement will be more rapid than ordinarily, if you allow him to move in and out, back and forth, to regress, to replenish his supplies.

Adam: Lily does that, working so hard at things which look simple to us, child's play, like throwing a ball and catching it and saying, "That's hard!"

Dr. Otto: You know, we wonder "How can that be hard?" For us, there's no effort extended, but for a child who's had the kinds of problems that Peter and Lily have had, that's hard work; just living is work. You're doing well with Lily. With Peter the attention span, the involvement is much shorter than it is for Lily; so much so that you have to try to interest him all the time, have cute or fascinating things to be used, but more than that, you will make use of the relationship which you will have with Peter and Peter will have with you, that will then allow him to become more extended in terms of his span of involvement. He's interested in snakes, and then he says, "I've had that." There are simpler activities to which he could revert, and you can make use of those simpler activities, which will allow him, as it will Lily, to move back into those more advanced things, like dinosaurs. Well, what happened after that little thing with the ruler?

Adam: Seemed to be okay.

Dr. Otto: That was also a clue you picked up that something was wrong.

Adam: In the situation, I probably should have helped him — the other ruler was in the drawer. We had been doing some measuring. The way I see it is that Peter has a number of small projects going on and I'm trying to keep up with them. One of them is measuring. Others are shapes, his interest in animals. I still think the snake is a shape.

Dr. Otto: That's right, it is. You might want to try and make use of this by actually getting models of dinosaurs from the Museum in Toronto.

Adam: The books just didn't work.

Dr. Otto: You need three-dimensional objects. If you can't get to Toronto, I'll go to the Museum and buy a series of the dinosaurs, they have small plastic models of all the different ones. What I suggest you do, when you have them, is just leave them around the room. Let him see that they are available, maybe help him to make almost a geological thing involving shapes, textures, involving him using the rest of the materials like sand, or clay, or papier-mâché. It will help him to try and combine the kinds of activities that he's doing, the measuring, the counting, the shapes. What we're going to try and do is really bring him together with three-dimensional objects.

Adam: He's also interested in the letters. They are shapes.

Dr. Otto: That's right. They are shapes. So he's really working on several different levels at the same time. Don't think of learning as linear, think of it as back and forth and curved. It's a nonlinear function.

Adam: It sort of moves.

Dr. Otto: And Peter's moving too.

Adam: I think it was on the same day as the ruler incident that he actually wanted to somehow write down letters. Probably his name. I wrote down all the letters, and he put the whole alphabet in his book. That's a really good start. The other thing that happened today was that he looked at all the shapes I have around the room. I have some fairly interesting ones. One of them was a pyramid but it had a right angle on it. He got quite involved in it. There was a rather plain shape, just a triangle. The one he liked was the three-dimensional one which has more depth. It would be more concrete. He liked that. He wanted to take it out and paint it, and so I said, "Okay, first let's try it on the corners," and we tried it different ways, and it did have a couple of right angles. Then he went out and painted it purple and it's sitting in the arts and crafts room. And then — I believe I drew something and cut it out, he wanted me to do that while he was there. He then got a triangular shape, traced it, and cut it out. He tried that in the corner and he put the shape together with the block. He said, "Hey, look at that!"

Dr. Otto: Oh, that's a marvellous way of learning. He's learning extra information.

Adam: It was terrific the way it happened. I felt I had manipulated him a little to trace it.

Dr. Otto: Well, you provided him with a model. You allowed him to imitate. You're setting the environment again for him to learn. That means you're changing it, altering it, adding in things so that it's going to be interesting, exciting, making him furious to go on and do the things that are going to be very helpful.

Adam: Since he had trouble entering things, I asked him if i could put his shape in his folder. And it's there now, and it was there when he opened it today. He sat down and looked around and then looked at his book. He also put some food in the drawer, a bag of Cheezies®, and he comes in and takes the bag out at various times.

Dr. Otto: He needs these supplies.

Adam: He's really designing his drawer quite a bit. I brought in one of the folding rules that open up in a zig-zag — it's a six-footer. I had brought it to measure the rug because I'm getting a pad for it. Lily was in there and as soon as I came in the door Peter said, "Can I use the ruler?" And I said, "Sure, bring it back later, I need it." They both helped to measure the rug, and Peter said, "Can I have this for the rest of the day?" "Yes," I replied, "Put it back in the drawer before you leave." Well, he left it at home so he didn't have it when he came in today. But I talked to him about the things he had measured.

Dr. Otto: He had gone about measuring things?

Adam: He measured the room and said it was ten feet, nine inches, which surprised me.

Dr. Otto: That's marvellous.

Adam: He could have said it was 7 feet. He may have had help from other people. We talked about the other things he had measured. Then he brought out a book. He happened to pick the simplistic dictionary. We sat down with it and used it in all kinds of ways for about half an hour, playing games like "I Spy." He said, "Will you read this book for me?" I said, "This isn't a reading book, it's a dictionary. We can find out about things." On one page there was an Indian. "That starts with an *I*." He said, "Well, let's look up some more." So he started to use the dictionary.

Dr. Otto: That's great. In terms of measuring you might want to put a piece of paper up, or put something up, on the wall that will allow him to, or allow you to, record some of the things he is measuring. It's not something that you have to deal with in an obtrusive way. You can put it up and put his name on it, and you can tell him he has done this and you will be recording the measurements for him.

Adam: That's a good idea, you know. Peter notices every change in the room. I had put up some photographs, pictures of kids doing things; they're quite nice. I took one off, to put one of Lily's up — she told me where to put it. She put up her pictures all over, like a little gallery. Peter looked at it and told me which ones he liked the best and he noticed one design had a face on it, that I hadn't even noticed.

Dr. Otto: He's really pretty perceptive. He's perceptive in terms of measuring, he's doing things with the ruler, he'll start to record them. I think this is coming along very nicely.

Adam: Today what happened with the letters of the alphabet happened in a very easy way. Peter didn't seem to get anxious or feel it was hard; he thought it was a game. I looked up "Indian" and he looked through pages for the pictures and he asked me to read what it said.

Dr. Otto: Well, that's important because he's telling you that

he is preparing himself to read, and he's working
with letters, he's working with shapes.

Adam: He would say, "I spy with my little eye, on this page,
something with this kind of shape and this kind of
colour." He said, "There's a design on the back of a
spider. It's yellow and it looks like a little girl with a
spot on her." And that's just what it looked like.
Mostly it's shapes he's telling me about. Sometimes
they are animals. He said once, "I spy something that
is black." He realized that it was kind of silly because
there were so many black letters there, but he said,
"There it is." He then said, "Now it's my turn." It
was always his turn.

We went on to talk about Allan, an older lad who wanted to
become involved in Adam's program, but who seemed to have
trouble getting his feet wet, so to speak. he definitely didn't like
the idea of making a book, said it was "Kid's stuff."

Dr. Otto: Try to find out what he's interested in, what specific
things he would like to do, not for his lifetime work,
but the concerns that he has now; then, on that basis,
hopefully, we will come up with something that's
interesting for him, not too difficult at first.

Adam: The tricky thing with these kids is what they consider to be simple things to learn.

Dr. Otto: It's very important to make them feel not ridiculous.
I mean it would be ridiculous to Allan to give him a
book like Cinderella. But what we will do is evolve a
project which needs a book and we will provide the
book, or he will, preferably he will go out and buy
the book and that's what all the information will be
placed in. It's a different kind of thing than Lily
would talk about or Peter would talk about.

Adam: Peter has been really excited about having liners —

Dr. Otto: That is not so exciting to Allan. It's threatening to
him. Those things point out that he can't do what he
should be doing or thinks he should be doing.

Adam: I need to have some more things to do. I think I can take on some more children. You know Rachel?

Dr. Otto: Yes, Talk to her and see whether she can use this.

Adam: — and Anne. She's an older girl, drifting right now, slips into drugs a lot, very depressed. That would make a big variety in ages.

Dr. Otto: That's fine. You interview Anne also and see how you think she would fit in. I don't mean with the rest of the children but into the program that you are trying to build.

Adam: I think she would be very difficult. I have already talked to her a little about it. She's really depressed.

Dr. Otto: She may not be prepared to deal with learning anything other than a relationship, but we certainly can provide her with a beginning of a relationship to help her relieve the depression and then, through that, go on and do whatever learning seems to be important for her.

Adam: It would be a good idea to do it in that way?

Dr. Otto: Yes. It's not going to be touching on loaded emotional material, it's much more going on to deal with the humanness of both of you.

Adam: She just sort of . . . just likes me. On the clean-up day she came in and sat in the chair very quietly.

The relationship Anne and Adam might evolve was an unknown quantity at this point. She was painfully depressed and, more than anything else, needed a relationship she could trust. We did not even concern ourselves with devising a project for her. The relationship was the project, I guess. The next week I arrived with the prehistoric animals for Peter.

Adam: Lily and I made some plans to go and see the horses. We had a regular session in the morning but we didn't really do much but talk about the trip. Anyway, we went, and she just walked one of the horses around. It's a very nice place. There's a young teenage girl there, Leslie, who has four horses: a colt, a brood mare, a thoroughbred, and a Shetland pony.

The Shetland pony is small like a dog, a pet. So Lily just walked it around. She didn't have any questions to ask, but I was asking the girl about the horses for my own information and I just left Lily to get to know the horse.

Dr. Otto: So Lily was with you when you were asking the questions, she could hear you.

Adam: I learned later that Lily has often played horse around the house and let people ride her. She's pretty involved in this horse thing. But the big thing was the arranging of it.

Dr. Otto: The arranging of it is part of the learning. It's very important she was able and allowed to do that. You can extend the seeing of the horses and the trip to the horses into all sorts of other projects; for instance, dealing with writing about horses. What is a brood mare, the whole pregnancy process, which I know nothing about. You may not know anything about it, it means you'll have to find out the information so you can help her.

Adam: That's why I was asking the questions. Lily got the names of the horses. I got quite a bit of information.

Dr. Otto: Well, that may all go into her book. She has all this information; you are extending this project from planning the visit to what you did, what you saw, not essentially making a nice story about what happened, but really doing it in terms of her interests in the whole thing.

Adam: She did some very nice organizing before, the morning we had our regular session. She looked at her notes, which were in outline form, and she took out a piece of paper and drew up another set of notes which were more concise. She picked out four or five areas of subject matter, and left room on the paper — she was going to take it with her to write things down.

Dr. Otto: Good. So she knows how to organize and order and classify. She's really organizing her own mind.

Adam: When she went she was pretty well organized, she had an idea of what she was going to do with her day, but I think she was just overwhelmed at the size, the smell of the horses, the whole thing was exciting for her; and she never really got to the questions. She heard me asking about what a colt was and she said, "Oh yeah, I was going to ask that."

Dr. Otto: You may want to make another visit, or more visits, there, to help her not to be so overwhelmed by everything.

Adam: That's why we had talked about going back. Leslie said we would be welcome to come back again.

Dr. Otto: Good. How's Peter?

Adam: For the first half hour there were so many things that we talked about. He lost my ruler, the folding one. I made up a little list and put down the things he had measured, including the ten foot, nine inch one. He had remembered all that quite well.

Dr. Otto: Did he do that by himself?

Adam: I don't know, I never found out.

Dr. Otto: It would be fascinating if he could do something as accurately as that. He'd have to do addition. This is really phenomenal.

Adam: I don't know where he got it, he must have done it with someone else. I told him I might get him a yardstick, then I went down to the hardware store and got him some free ones, so he can lose these as much as he wants.

Dr. Otto: I see your method. Every place he bumps into there will be a yardstick.

Adam: The folding one is in the house, but we can't find it. He's very picky about what goes into his book. Really, nothing can go in there very easily. He had some Sesame Street books and I noticed something with numbers on it, large numbers that could be cut out: it's like a puzzle — it was a big poster with numbers, three watermelons and three stickers. I cut it out and he put it together. It was easy to do but quite satisfying to finish. Then he wanted to tape it together to keep it that way but I reminded him that then it wouldn't be a puzzle any longer, it would be solid. He thought that out for a minute and said, "I would like to tape the pieces together and put them on a piece of paper," so I helped him to do that; it took quite a bit of time.

Dr. Otto: And he was able to stay with it and to do it in an organized way?

Adam: We were at it for over an hour.

Dr. Otto: That's lovely.

Adam: We were quite involved. It was the first time I was being critical at all. I helped him trace a finger puppet, and he started cutting it out, he looked at me and I said, "You didn't do a good job, did you?" He seemed to be able to accept that very nicely.

Dr. Otto: It's okay as long as you criticize a specific act rather than the child. And certainly I don't think we can let something go by when, really, the child knows. . . .

Adam: Then he did cut it out quite nicely, and in a really skillful way. The construction paper didn't hold together, so we had to tape it, but otherwise the puzzle was very nice. There's an interesting thing that happened with the six and the nine on the number puzzle —

Dr. Otto: Reversals?

Adam: Well, the six and nine were the same. On the little bits, on the bottom was written nine in letters. He wasn't really paying much attention to those. I pointed out that the six and the nine were quite alike and asked which one would he like to have. He just picked one. He didn't pick the six for the nine, you know, upside down. That wasn't a problem for him.

Dr. Otto: But by your pointing out different things in his world, he becomes more aware of it and he begins to learn, so you're functioning, again, as a catalyst. You're saying to yourself, "What is this kid about, what does he comprehend from me if I talk to him and if I give him instructions?"

Adam: If I had gone further and said, "If you put this on a page, the nine will be upside down," that would have been meaningless to him. I just played with the shapes, which was what we were talking about. The two shapes were similar and interchangeable.

Dr. Otto: He was playing with the shapes when he was doing the jigsaw puzzle and he put them together, with symmetry, so the whole thing is fitting into the way in which we are talking about the learning for Peter.

Adam: And that goes along with the dinosaurs. I was thinking dinosaurs for him belonged more to the idea of shapes than to the idea of dinosuars per se or anything to do with prehistory. It's their shapes he's interested in, so the three-dimensional ones are much more appropriate. He'll be able to use them.

Dr. Otto: You are introducing them into your learning environment in a way that maybe he can make sense of and use. It means not just telling him that how he has dinosaurs and we are going to do this and that with them, but trying to think where he is at with them, why they are there for him, and trying to extend the project so that you can bring these models into the "now" in a way that makes sense to Peter. Okay now, what's happened with Allan?

Adam: I talked to him some more about meeting and getting on with the reading he says he wants to learn, and he seemed quite pleased that I would be around, and if he ever wanted to do anything he would let me know.

Dr. Otto: He knows that you're there and you're not pushing him away and you're available. Okay — the two new ones, Anne and Rachel.

Rachel started off as both Lily and Peter had: Adam gave her a binder and paper so she could start making a book. She seemed very anxious, as if it were a "school thing," and that she had to do something very special. Like Lily, she too was interested in horses. She did a bit of tracing and colouring — both she and

Adam agreed it looked a little funny. Adam felt she'd had enough for one day, but no, Rachel wanted to do some writing. She felt she had to do everything, not out of a natural curiosity or desire to do, but from a compulsion. She tried to do a lot of things that first session, attempting things that were too difficult for her, trying to write everything, in essence, trying to cope with a desire to please.

Adam: The next week she came in she remembered about the coloured paper I had shown her and started doing something a little more her own speed. She wanted to draw a barn because she had written about a barn; she was talking about horses but she was writing about a barn.

   I asked her if she had ever cut out pieces of paper and stuck it on other pieces of paper. She said, "Yes, that's a good idea." So she started to make a barn out of pieces of paper. She put this triangular piece in red for the barn and I helped her, showed her how to glue it. She put it on and I said, "Would you like to press that down?" because I remember Peter had such a big time jumping up and down on the book, pressing it. I picked out a shape: I wasn't really thinking about it consciously, but I picked out the same triangular shape to fit right on the top and I noticed it as soon as I gave it to her — she said, "Whoa, we got the same shape." She pressed on it and I got out a few other shapes that were similar to the other ones she was pasting on, and she got along pretty well with the pasting and pressing.

Dr. Otto: Good.

Adam: Then right in front of her, I took a rectangular solid block, and on the top of it I put the triangular one; she looked up and said, "That's a barn." I was collecting little bits and pieces and I had a paper towel roll which I put next to it. She said, "That's the thing, you know, what is it called?" She talked a little bit about it and I said "It's called a silo."

Dr. Otto: Lovely. You extended her project. She's excited and learning.

Adam: Yes, she was really excited. She kept saying how much fun she was having. She was much more re-laxed, doing something she could do. She wanted to write "barn" at the top and without any prompting at all she got her book and went along until she got to the word *barn* and spelt "barn" at the top. I also sprinkled the reinforcements out because· they were shapes that she could get interested in making some-thing out of, but she backed off. It was a little too far out or something.

Dr. Otto: It was a little too complicated — she's learning how to spell, she's reading and doing and is involved in the things we think of as a project.

Adam: She'll be very good because she seems to be —

Dr. Otto: Capable of being involved in an interesting program?

Adam: Yes.

Dr. Otto: You know, I think we should suggest to some people that they collect junk material for you.

Adam: Yes — the art room needs a lot more things — a lot of the things we can get don't cost anything, we can get scraps. The kids collect a lot of odds and ends, like paper towels, bits of cloth. I've also got different-shaped jars that have the same volume.

Dr. Otto: Right. You're going to teach them conserva-tion.

Adam: Anyway, that's where Rachel is and that's very exciting for me. Now with Anne, it's the first time I have seen her, and she is a very depressed girl.

Dr. Otto: She's the adolescent.

Adam: She's seventeen. It has taken her a few weeks to fi-nally arrange a time with me. One day she asked me and I said, "We'll do it this afternoon." She's taking correspondence courses and there was an English lesson on a short story she was to read with questions to be answered, and she wanted me to do a lot of it. She was rather anxious about this work. I learned later that she has expressed a lot of concern about being behind in school — that's why she's taking the courses. The problem, it turned out, was her writing things down, this was really where she balked. We talked about it, about the questions and so on, and what with mixing her ideas and mine, we got a lot done. But when it came to putting down the answers to numbers one, two, and three, it was tricky. So I tried to help her be more flexible and to skip number one, that didn't have to be done first, you know. "Why don't you pick the one that's most interesting to you?" is what I said, and so number two is the one that we talked about the most. We went on to number three, and we had the answer to number one out of that. I pointed that out to her. At that point I spoke to her about how things were going, and I said, "It's okay when you and I talk, we get ideas and find out a lot of things about the story, but when we try to write them down, it's very hard"; so I encouraged her to write down just short phrases rather than —

Dr. Otto: Yes, rather than some paragraph.

Adam: Yes, I had the idea that she wanted to have it down "good" is the way she said it: "Well, I'll do it in good later." So I said, "Well, you don't have to do it in good until later, that's true, but sometimes it's sort of hard to just write something down quickly in a sloppy way, it doesn't look so nice on the paper, but it's a good way to get your ideas down quickly. It would be very hard if we always had to put our ideas into perfect sentences all the time."

Dr. Otto: You have caught on beautifully: I mean you really have the essence of what we have been talking about in terms of meeting the needs of the children: understanding what is happening to the child, recognizing peculiar problems that they have, and not pushing them beyond the point where we would like to eventually see them, but making sure that they are ready for what you are approaching them with. I'm really happy, I think this is extremely exciting.

Adam: Well, we went along and she did manage to do that, and she was quite pleased to see how much she could actually write when it didn't have to be "in good." She was going to do "in good" later, she had had enough; and I said, "Yes, you worked really hard today." She was almost perspiring. It was really quite an effort to do it. I said that we would do one next week. Now, there's another problem I think. Anne's been dabbling three hours a day, nearly, on this correspondence course. I don't think she's ready to handle it. If there is a deadline on it she probably won't be able to manage it.

Dr. Otto: You're right.

Adam: She works pretty hard for those three hours, and it turns out her teacher does most of it for her.

Dr. Otto: Yes, so that it only reinforces Anne's view that she's pretty bad.

Adam: Evidently, someone heard Anne make a remark, sort of "Adam doesn't do very much for me" . . .

Dr. Otto: Right — that's not a negative thing at all.

Adam: I know.

Dr. Otto: It's really important that we don't push Anne, or help her too much. At this point she isn't able to respond to that kind of help, and to push her is only to continue the kinds of problems she has with feeling she's not able to do things, that she's not able to please, that she's essentially a bad person. Be careful you don't do too much for her because this is only telling her "You're no good." She has a problem and we have to live with the problem at the rate at which she can advance.

Adam: She's already done a lot of things with John, with painting, he's an artist; and she's really enjoyed it, but I think she might do a few other kinds of things along the same line.

Dr. Otto: She'll recognize you as a teacher, the one who helps her, who's able to stimulate her, and can recognize how fast she can or cannot travel; who encourages her, but doesn't really demand and doesn't do things for her, and in this way you'll really help her whole self-image "Who am I?" and "How do I feel about

myself? and can I accomplish something?" Surely
during that session she had with you, she was able to
recognize that she did a lot. You created a background for her and she was able to work in the fore-
ground, and that's really tremendous.

We got off on a tangent her — Anne had been uncomfortable
sitting on the floor and Adam decided he needed some tables
and chairs. It would make an ideal project for some of the
children, for it served a real need as opposed to some woodworking project geared to simply making objects at random.
We discussed "finishing" projects, something that had both-
ered Adam for a long time and a bone of contention among
many who work with children.

Adam: . . . that bothers me, you know, the idea of finishing
           something. There can be a lot of pressure for the
           child to finish the project, the candlestick holder, or
           the table, or whatever. Even if the project began with
           the child's interest, he was motivated to start some-
           thing; then there's pressure to finish it. In other
           words there has to be this —
Dr. Otto: Yes, well, there's a moral value. I think whether they
           complete the project, and how they complete it, is to
           a large extent up to the way in which we create the
           environment. If you force a child to finish the project
           at that time, at our time, then what you will really
           encourage is that the child be hostile, and you en-
           courage a kind of acting out, either destroying the
           project, or destroying something else that perhaps is
           important.
Adam: Yes, there is a lot of worry about things getting dam-
           aged in the school, you know.
Dr. Otto: But this is precisely one of the reasons why things get
           damaged in schools. For instance, you talked about
           the record player.
Adam: About worrying about it being damaged —
Dr. Otto: Yes, and one of the reasons why it could be damaged
           is because a teacher, an adult, will say "Oh, don't

play that record, I don't like it" — it's their point of
view, not the child's. So you know they are really, in
a sense, without recognizing it, encouraging a kind
of acting out on the very aspects they are concerned
about.

Adam: That's really good — I hadn't pulled it together like
that, I hadn't made the connections.

The next time we met we had a long talk about Peter. He was
moving ahead at a furious pace, too fast perhaps, but neverthe-
less it was his rhythm and all we could do was run along with
him. It was breathtaking to be involved with him.

Adam: Peter did quite a bit. I gave him a yardstick and
I noticed he was measuring things around the
room. When he first came in he said to me, "I don't
know what to do today." He's done that before — I
just sit down when he does that and chat with
him.

Dr. Otto: Does your chatting with him move in the direction of
the projects that he has already?

Adam: Yes. I ask him about his dinosaurs, if he's been
playing with them. With him, it's the dinosaurs and
the measuring, really, at this point but he didn't
want to do anything with those interests right then,
he wanted to read a book. After that, he started
making faces. We have a mirror in there and I encourage him, so he made some faces in the mirror. I
came back to the dinosaurs again — he said he's been
playing with them and I think he said something
like, "I eat and fight." Pretty simply, that's about all
he was saying and he didn't want to do too much
with that. Anyway, to get back to the measuring, he
got a little frustrated handling the yardstick on his
own, but he can measure things and he even knows
halves, he can say, "16 and 1/2 inches."

Dr. Otto: So he could read it off the yardstick.

Adam: We talked about the yardstick and I had noted that he
could do the half inches, so I got his binder out and I

asked Peter if it was all right for me to have put that thing in his binder.

Dr. Otto: Which thing?

Adam: The page with his measurements on it. I checked it out because I felt that I had sort of pushed it into his binder, and that binder is pretty touchy with Peter, so I was feeling a little funny about it. I told him that I had been excited about his measuring and that I had put it in his binder last week. He said, "Oh, yeah, that's fine." So we measured some more things and wrote them down; he measured and I wrote them down.

Dr. Otto: Does he talk about doing anything with these numbers? Does he talk about the measurements? What does he do after you have written them down? Does it finish at that point, or what happens?

Adam: He doesn't do too much with them right away. What happened was that I had a list of about six numbers, and then he wanted to measure the rug; and it was longer than the yardstick so he needed some help with that, and asked me for it. I showed him how to do it and he counted off, put down 36, and then I put his finger there and moved the ruler up and counted off the rest to 47 1/2.

Dr. Otto: So he added on from 36, by counting each unit.

Adam: By counting each unit, he just took it one by one. But it seems to me that he is able to read off the ruler what number it is, he's able to say that's 24, without counting.

Dr. Otto: He knows his numbers?

Adam: He knows his numbers.

Dr. Otto: Up to a point — we don't know what point. Now he has counted the units and added the 36, making 47, one of the things you can do is to put 36 down on the paper and say, "We counted 11 units and see, here's the 36 down here, and then we'll put down the 11 units and that comes out to the total, the sum of what you said, 47.

Adam: I did that verbally and I did something like that in the book. I talked to him about how we had added on some other numbers because the yardstick wasn't long enough. He seemed to understand that — but it was hard to understand, and when that happens, he always asks me to do something.

Dr. Otto: Well, you tell him that it's a hard thing to do and it will take him a little while to really master it.

Adam: Right, that's the sort of thing I said. I said, "I'd be glad to measure something. Do you have anything in mind?" He said, "No," and I said, "How about if I measure you?" So I lined him up against the wall and made a mark and measured him. Of course he had a yardstick too, and that's what I had in mind. So he again got involved in adding.

Dr. Otto: That's good. That does several things, and one of the things that we really want to help Peter with, and what he was doing in the mirror, is finding out who he really is; those faces that he makes are really just, "How much can I really distort myself, and how far can I extend myself, and what am I able to do?" He really has to learn more about himself, and I think that it gradually comes out. It's giving him more of an idea of his own body image: how big he is, where he extends to in terms of inches, in whatever measurement unit you are using.

Adam: — and as a comparison to other things, I said he was much bigger than the picture, and things like that.

Dr. Otto: So he becomes bigger than certain things and smaller than others; and then you are moving again into the kind of classification of bigger and smaller and that, along with the measuring you're doing, will help him to get the whole concept of what is number and what is measurement. It's not so much that we're just adding one and one to make two, we're not just trying to do it by rote, but just in a simple way, to add one and one. Children can do this, but what we want for Peter is to give him an underlying understanding, a concept of what is measurement; and that involves not just the number per se but the whole orientation of the numbering, like bigger and smaller, less and more, higher and lower, all these things which are very important. Measurement comes in in the sense of measuring with two pails or two bottles; you know, is this bottle more than this bottle, does it contain more? If they are both the same, if both have the same amount in them and they are different shapes, does it still mean that they are the same amount?

Adam: Do you think Peter is ready for something like that?

Dr. Otto: Yes. You could set your environment so that you would encourage him to do this kind of measuring. The thing that you might also want to try is find a scale — not a bathroom scale, because it isn't sufficiently balanced. Get a butcher's scale where you have a platform and you can put things on it, something that measures up to ten or twenty pounds, where you can read off the weight on a pointer and when you have two pieces as opposed to one piece, these kinds of things. I'm not sure where you can get one —

Adam: I have a friend that has one.

Dr. Otto: Great, borrow it.

Adam: Some of the other things that happened are interesting as well. He found some maracas in the bottom drawer and started dancing around and shaking them to a definite rhythm; I was able to clap the rhythm, and he danced around for a while and was really delighted by that. It seemed to me that this time he did a number of things. He seemed to be quite fluid. Before, he would be a little more rigid and lost. He is getting a little freer with me. And he sees it's all right to dance and enjoy himself.

Dr. Otto: One of the errors I think most of our school systems have created is the assumption that learning goes on in little bits and pieces. I think that learning is a whole flowing sequence, everything comes together. It's not just "Now we do this," but it really means setting a stage so that the whole child's life goes and flows. Along with it, you have made the environment so that math and reading all become part of it, they are not something extra, away from; they are meaningful to the child, and that's what you are doing in your room. That's what Peter is really showing you. It's a flow, it's not a small, specific act that is supposed to be learned, and it means that learning is a sequence of flowing through, it takes the rhythm that the child takes and it can't be unnatural. You must be aware of when the child is ready to participate — that is one of the most difficult things in teaching. The child can say, "I'm ready." The teacher can say, "I'm not, so wait," and that's ludicrous, but that is what happens.

Adam: That's crazy!

Dr. Otto: Is there anything else that Peter is doing that we should talk about?

Adam: He looked at the books again after he danced around; he went out and got one and I was thinking that probably I should end it there because he had done quite a bit, but I think reading a book was a nice way of ending it. The book was *The Sorcerer's Apprentice*, and I read that to him. He wanted to know what an apprentice was and I tried to explain it to him. He said that he would like to be a singer. I said, "Well, who's your favourite singer?" and he said, "Elvis Pretzel." So I talked to him about what his duties would be to Elvis Pretzel in return for teaching him to sing.

Adam was ready to close the session, but Peter wanted another book read, this one on Indians (Pocahontas). This in turn sparked a request to be taken to an Indian village. Adam told him about the Huron Village in Midland, and as he and I discussed the trip, another project for Peter was on its way. There was a whole world of "Indian" for him: the music and the kind of dancing he was doing, the rhythm, the numbers involved for the trip (how far, what time, how long, etc.). This branches out into helping him to become interested in geography, mathematics, in social studies, because that is the Indian, and on top of it all, like an umbrella, the reading. Marvellous project!

Adam: Okay — now that takes care of Peter. The others — I'll start off with Amelia. Oh, I didn't tell you, she's a new one with me —

Dr. Otto: Good. I know her.

Adam: This was the first time we'd been together, and she wanted to do math; she wanted me to write some questions down and she'd fill in the answers. I gradually made the questions a little harder, and we talked about what she could do. She was able to add up quite long lists of numbers, and carry her numbers.

Dr. Otto: So she's able to add four numbers?

Adam: Yes, or even more, it makes no difference; and she's able to put in commas.

Dr. Otto: How old is Amelia again?

Adam: She's nine.

Dr. Otto: And she's using commas, and she's understanding the addition? That's excellent.

Adam: She has quite a bit of background on this. We did a lot of working with numbers and shapes — matching numbers and shapes together.

Dr. Otto: Ah yes, so she's really becoming symbolic.

Adam: Yes, I think so. We did a whole bunch of them and it was really neat the way it went. We put them in her binder. It's quite a nice big page full. After that I said, "Do you know anything about fractions?" That didn't seem to make any sense to her. I said, "Can you fold a piece of paper in half?" So I got a piece of paper and she folded it in half, and I wrote on one side "1/2" and she looked at it for awhile and then we started talking about how it might fit into the whole, so that's as far as we went. It went pretty concretely.

Dr. Otto: Yes, exactly.

Adam: It all seemed to be a bit much for her; we dropped it and talked about wanting to draw houses, and I was amazed at how terrible she was at drawing after all this math. She drew a very crude house with a double door on it — she's interested in that. So I suggested that she cut some paper up and make it another way. She picked only one colour, orange, and did the whole thing in orange, and then she drew some people; but the roof of the house wasn't connected, and the shapes were very crude, the tree was just a big clump with a little tiny thing at the top.

Dr. Otto: Think of her as really being a pretty disconnected child, like her world isn't connected. She's pretty mixed up emotionally. If I say she's a pretty fragmented child, I mean that her ego is just bits and pieces all over the place. Numbers mean something to her in the sense that she can put them together, and she can make sense out of those numbers. Now when it comes to something emotional, when it comes to something interpersonal like the drawing of the house, things that could be emotionally charged for her, Amelia has a little more difficulty. Gradually you'll find that this will change. She will become more organized and her interests will extend to more areas, like Peter's. Then she'll be able to explore her areas of deficiencies and she'll go on to things that are more difficult, harder for her to deal with.

Adam: Lily made a catalogue this week — a people's catalogue and chose pictures she liked, cut them out and I just sat back and watched her and she made a whole catalogue. Apparently she has used it quite a bit, has made up her own order blanks, which I introduced. This is the front page. She put this little thing here.

Dr. Otto: "Love makes people happy."

Adam: She was pretty excited about that and she had me classify the pictures later on, put them together, order them and put them back in the book. We numbered the pages too. She has her catalogue.

Dr. Otto: Good, so you're numbering, writing, you're doing all sorts of things. How old is Lily again?

Adam: She's eleven.

Dr. Otto: . . . and she's able to do these things with skill.

Adam: She's also still interested in the horses — we are going to go this week. She'll just have to go and look at the horses again and maybe sit on one; it is pretty important to her, she thinks of herself as a horse, in a way.

Dr. Otto: Yes, but she's beginning to see that maybe she is more than a horse. I mean, she's got a catalogue and at least now she can start cataloguing to find out, "Who could I be? What could I do? What could I wear? What could I buy?"

Adam: That is just exactly what she does. She's really ordering things very nicely, very rapidly from where we started.

Dr. Otto: Oh, very, very good.

Adam: Well, it was the second time I had seen Anne — you remember the things we did, with her course?

Dr. Otto: Yes, the correspondence course.

Adam: Well, she didn't make it up to see me and I went looking for her; I saw that she was sitting all alone in the living room knitting, and I said that it was okay for her to come up and do her knitting, so she came up. I said, "I have some other things to do," and I made as if I were sorting out my brief case and things like that. We just started talking, and it turned out she was very interested in horses too. She wasn't too interested in finding any books on them, but she wanted to learn how to ride one, so I mentioned that Lily and I would be visiting a farm and if she would like to come along, it would be okay. I have a feeling Lily would like someone else along, too. The next subject she brought up was that she wanted something to read besides her correspondence course. I talked to her about books and it turned out that she was interested in biographies. She had read a book by Steinbeck and *The Lord of the Rings*. I think the next thing we are going to do is go to the library.

Dr. Otto: Going to the library would be very good for Anne, especially if you help to choose books that are going to be fascinating to her, and that she's going to want to read completely; not that we want her to finish the reading per se, it's more that we want to help her to recognize her "thing" in this reading, her interest in the reading.

At our next session, before we started talking about the children, we discussed a film we had just seen.

Dr. Otto: I wonder if teachers really recognize that unless the child is able to accept, understand, and is ready to begin to learn, no matter how much teaching you try to push into the child, the child just doesn't seem to grasp the concept. If that point came through in the film, it was good, but I think it's missing a great deal in terms of what children are like, and how you talk to children. I don't think that the approach in the film was at all effective.

Adam: I thought it gave me a look at a so-called normal situation. I have a hard time understanding the relationship between our kids' disturbances and the problems they have with learning and dealing with me, compared with normal children.

Dr. Otto: I think that one of the things is that the problems the child has prevent him from really understanding, grasping or retaining the kind of instruction you are giving. So what you have to work on first is really an ego relationship between you and the child that essentially will remove the emotional blocks to what you are saying. Because there is a safety involved in the relationship, there is an understanding and a sensitivity on your part, and you know just exactly how much the child is ready to accept, what his needs are, the way we've been talking about things in terms of the interest of the child and using that as a motivating factor. You work from a base of a relationship, from the readiness of a child, from the motivational system you understand. Now, I don't think that's a bad base or a poor base or an inadequate base to work from with any child, normal or disturbed.

Adam: But a normal child could go about learning and doing a lot more even if he didn't know the teacher, and then you wouldn't need that kind of base.

Dr. Otto: You're right — he would learn more if he knew the teacher and if he had a good relationship with the teacher; but regardless, he would still learn. He would learn slower, and one of the things we find with normal children is that they often fantasize a relationship between themselves and the teacher and they talk about the teacher, in a fantasy way, in a positive fantasy way, particularly if they are doing okay.

Adam: How much of a relationship do they really have in a day with thirty-five kids? You know, the films and books we see are mainly about primary education; one of the concerns of the schools, not necessarily mine, is what to do with the older children. What I think is needed at the school is to take a more stringent look at the children individually.

Dr. Otto: Right.

Adam: When we get going on that, then what we look at we can offer the older children.

Dr. Otto: What you are saying is that you and the staff, the teachers should get together to talk about each child and the needs of each child, so that you can really individualize what's going on.

Adam: That's what I was going to ask you about.

Dr. Otto: I think it's a very important recommendation in terms of understanding, for instance, what is a thirteen-year-old, what does he need? What does a fifteen-year-old need in terms of where he is at? Looking at the child individually is very important.

Adam: The one thing that I think is invaluable is to talk about the children and not about ideas.

Dr. Otto: Yes. If you focus more on specific children and the specific needs and readiness of each child, I think everyone will get a lot more than if you talk about abstract ideas.

Adam: Right. There's a need for abstract ideas, but only as a base from which you consider the specific child without bringing in the authoritarian, saying, for example, "He should be doing this now," "She should be more advanced at this point," "You're late, get here on time." It takes a long time to change from that authoritarian attitude, because you can't just say, "Stop being authoritarian."

Dr. Otto: Right. You have to have patience, but I think you also have to build something into the environment that allows the change to begin, to see that there is something else that can go on. There's another way of living. Generally, the schools don't see it yet. It's modelling. It's providing yourself, other teachers and the system with an alternate way of working with children. I don't think that what we, (you and I) are doing here is creating some kind of revolution, but I think we are really only extending our thinking so that we can approach children from different points of view. All children are not the same, therefore, you must approach children flexibly. Okay — let's talk about your children.

Adam was quite excited about Amelia. After her rather primitive attempt at drawing a house, she turned out to be extremely clever at manoeuvering some blocks Adam gave her. She constructed a really fabulous house, painting the blocks in beautiful colours, developing a modernistic and quite complicated design. She seemed freer to investigate things, to make use of her creativity. She was still involved in her math, but she saw that more as "school work," taking her exercises home to have someone mark them.

Rachel was evolving a project, a minature farmyard and

garden. She was growing seeds which she wanted to plant in bottle caps, and then put the caps in a box with little fences around them. It was a fascinating project, with small buildings, and involved chickens and eggs which branced out into selling the eggs to feed the horses, so we were studying the pricing of eggs and the cost of feed, dealing with fractions and concepts of dozens and so on.

Adam: I took Lily and Anne to see the horses Wednesday. It was a very cold day and Anne couldn't stay outside for very long. The horses frightened Lily again. They frightened Anne too. The girls had ideas of horses as beautiful pets, but when they got closer, they were quite frightened.

Dr. Otto: That's really much more — it's their fantasies, you know, about what's going on.

Adam: That's right, so this process is making it more real. Lily was quite upset. The cause of it was the little Shetland pony; I think it really stayed away from her. She didn't like that at all and went to see Jack and Jill, two Chinese geese; one of them attacked her and bit her coat, and she was really frightened.

Dr. Otto: Yes, it would be quite frightening to anybody.

Adam: Anne went inside, she was so cold and frightened. I don't know if she was more frightened or more cold. We fed the horse some water and they drank buckets at a time, which was kind of neat.

Dr. Otto: They have such an enormous water appetite.

Adam: I was concerned about where this project was going to go with Lily, because she was so satisfied in some ways. When we got back, when she came for her regular time on Friday she was still interested in horses and we talked about some of the things that had happened. The horse she was most frightened of was the thoroughbred called Alice deBred, actually a race horse, and we talked about thoroughbreds. We looked up the word in the dictionary; she has a way of reading things that she doesn't really comprehend, I think I told you that. She had a hard time using the dictionary, but we've been using it quite regularly and she's gotten a little better, and we wanted to look up "thoroughbred" in the encyclopedia. There was a nice little display in it with some diagrams that she traced.

Dr. Otto: She made her own display?

Adam: Yes, one of the central nervous system, and a skeleton we talked about a little. She's able to read the rather complicated text but doesn't understand a whole lot. Certain words interested her, and how a thoroughbred came about; you know, a mixture of an Arabian and an English horse. We talked about ancestors and descendants and things like that.

Dr. Otto: She's learning about genetics.

Adam: Yes. Another thing she has learned are diagrams. She wanted to know what a certain drawing was, and I said it was called a diagram. She was keeping a few little notes which were going to go into her book as well as the diagram she'd traced. She went ahead, just like a real scholar, had her notebook out and paper and books. I extended her diagram a little and talked to her about her family; and we started a family tree.

Dr. Otto: Oh, good! I would suggest that if it is at all possible and practical, you actually go through generations and show her how you breed in or breed out some things genetically. You can do this with guppies, you can take two guppies and then the female has babies; when they're grown up you can match a daughter with the father and you can start changing the colours of the tail, the spots and things like that. I think that guppies breed about every three weeks. If there is a faster breeding animal, maybe mice, take a black and a white and breed them. I think their gestation period is eighteen days; that way you can actually begin to show her how genetics and a thoroughbred theme works. I think you should talk about it at fair length with her before you just jump into it.

Adam: Yes, that's right. Peter arrived when we were fin-
           ishing up. I didn't get the scale for him, I hope to get
           it this weekend.

Peter was still on his learning rampage. They began using
some bottles Adam had saved, measuring levels of water in
each, pouring water from a fat bottle into a tall thin one, seeing
the different levels and understanding different shapes.

Adam: On Friday I took Anne to the library. She wanted to
           find *The Lord of the Rings*, but they were out of it. I
           showed her how to use the card catalogue; it turned
           out she didn't know too much about how to use a
           library and we looked up the book and saw it was
           gone. The librarian suggested that we look on the
           rack, in the paperback section. There was a book by
           the same author, *The Hobbit*, so we looked into the
           preface to that and she was very pleased to take it —
           that's the only book she wanted.
Dr. Otto: Fine.
Adam: I left her alone while she got her library card; she had
           a very difficult time with it, she couldn't answer any
           of the librarian's questions, like "What's you phone
           number?" "What school do you go to?" and things
           like that. She called me over and I had to answer for
           her — she was feeling a little uncomfortable about
           that. Anne is seventeen and she's very depressed. She
           seems to be a little bored, a little frustrated.
Dr. Otto: Think of the boredom and the kind of frustration
           you see in her as signs of her depression. Not so
           much boredom as you and I might describe it,
           though that may also be part of her depression, but
           really, with her, it's a symptom of her depression.
Adam: So doing more things —
Dr. Otto: Will help her become more involved, help her to
           recognize how she is gaining from the things she's
           doing now. She is the kind of person who doesn't
           think she gets much out of anything.
Adam: I had a good talk with her school staff about her
           school program. They're not going to push her about

the correspondence course. She got a 60 in English. That's okay, really, but she seemed a little disappointed.

Dr. Otto: She feels she's a failure generally.

Adam: Yes. Right. I told them that she would not be able to accept a high grade anyway.

Dr. Otto: It's hard to accept a low grade and hard to accept a high grade.

Adam: But after we went to the library I took a look at some magazines and she wanted to look at some of the pretty girls in *Seventeen*; when I took her home we sat and chatted a little and made some tea. So I am sort of being a friend to her.

Dr. Otto: You're a friend and a teacher and I think the friend will help the teacher.

Adam discussed Peter and Rachel briefly and then, again, presented his old quandary, the question of finishing.

Adam: It was interesting, Amelia said, "I want to work with wood this week." I had a whole drawer full of blocks and she really enjoys those. She made a house and a sea — she really likes working with wood. She said, "I don't like going down to the basement to work with wood" and I said, "Why not?" You know it's too hard, if we work upstairs, to get everything we need, we have to keep running up and down the stairs. She said she couldn't go down there, or work down there, because she had something she hadn't finished and she wasn't allowed to start anything else until she finished that.

Dr. Otto: Oh, I see.

Adam: So this little girl hasn't used the basement for some time now.

Dr. Otto: Well, that's a shame. It's sad, because that's a pretty good way of turning her off from doing something, by insisting that something be finished.

Adam: There are ways to help someone finish; it's nice for kids to finish things, but there are ways to do it. I get the idea that it's terrifically satisfying for kids to finish something, for the child —

Dr. Otto: Not for the adult? There's something in it for the adult too, the satisfaction of being able to demonstrate, "I started this with you and I finished this with you."

Adam: But you don't want all this unfinished junk lying around.

Dr. Otto: Well, maybe we could look at it this way . . . kids might be able to come back to projects, particularly if you don't insist they finish right away. Generally, if you leave the environment so that when the child goes away from it he knows what he's left, he will return to it if you really haven't upset it or disturbed it; but if you make all sorts of rules and regulations about how you are to do things and when you are to finish things, I think you will find that kids will resist it. Their resistance will be expressed by incompletion.

Adam: Well, then probably that has become an issue because of the necessity for each child to be with an adult, just not free.

Dr. Otto: I can understand the danger of power tools with children who are impulsive; they have to have a place where there are no power tools. That's exactly what you do: you permit the child to go into an area where he may not want to use power tools, at this point.

Adam: You know what power tools are like. They're loud. Eric just cut his hand.

Dr. Otto: Who did?

Adam: Eric ———.

Dr. Otto: I didn't know he hurt himself.

Adam: A lot of kids had a reaction to that. The woodworking shop isn't a place to play, in other words, that is why there is a lot of resistance to getting very simple projects done.

Dr. Otto: I think for younger children —

Adam: They don't go down there at all.

Dr. Otto: They should be permitted to, and encouraged to, but there shouldn't be these expensive, powerful, electrical tools; I think we should have hammers and saws and screwdrivers and nails. They would get a lot of pleasure from that.

Adam: They cut up the blocks in my drawer and make stacks of wood.

Dr. Otto: They'll pound pieces together and they'll make boats out of them; and they'll paint their boats and they'll learn shapes and learn power, their own power. Well, I'm not sure how you will be able to handle the basement, but it sounds like the basement is a scary place and that's too bad, because psychologically the basement is a place where we want the children to dump out things and get rid of their feelings, which are really down in their "basement." If that powerful tool, which they have no control over and can't master, is down there, then I think that psychologically it's a pretty conflicting situation as though the child were saying. "I want to go down, but I'm afraid to stay there because I don't know what will happen." The child has no control over these powerful machines.

Adam: No, that's true.

Dr. Otto: And psychologically he is not being permitted the chance to gain control over these powerful things, from both views: from an educational view, from a psychological point of view; and also from a third point, from an interpersonal point of view. You said that there are two children you are having some trouble with?

Adam: Amelia and Peter are going along pretty well. I don't think I need to see them more than once a week. Anne is doing just about nothing but looking for a concert to go to in Toronto. That's about where she is.

Dr. Otto: And emotionally isn't that about all she can do, also?

Adam: How?

Dr. Otto: Emotionally, is she prepared to, is she able to, is she

ready to cope with other kinds of things than the idea
of planning concerts or planning to go to concerts?

Adam: She's hardly able to do that.

Dr. Otto: So that expecting her to do more would really be an
error?

Adam: That's right. We're just keeping in touch and talking
about what concerts there are. So then Rachel built a
little farm and painted it.

Dr. Otto: You've bought the seeds?

Adam: Yes. She saw a blue circle that was in the drawer and
she wanted to make a pond out of it. We planted the
seeds — that was a week ago on Friday.

Dr. Otto: Are they sprouting at all?

Adam: Well, she's been watering them and looking after
them. I don't know how it's going to go, but there
are some sprouts, she reported to me last night.

Dr. Otto: Lovely, thank goodness!

Adam: Yes. Evidently oats will grow any place. They are
like weeds, but the other things are a little more
delicate so we might just get some oats. I wasn't sure
where to go from there. On Thursday she came in at
the end of Lily's appointment and we wound up
playing store.

Dr. Otto: Did your store involve the sale of merchandise or the
setting up of a store?

Adam: It was a restaurant. I wrote a menu on the board and
asked Rachel what the prices might be and she did
some really strange things with it. A small coke was
45 cents, a large coke was 25 cents. The small one
cost more than the big one. It was as though she
wasn't really —

Dr. Otto: She wasn't attuned to the pricing.

Adam: We had started off in a very concrete way with her
making pictures, making this farm, but it's hard to
find out what some of her abilities are.

Dr. Otto: And you find that they are pretty much at a low level.

Adam: Yes; you know, the small coke cost more than the
large coke.

Dr. Otto: What you have now is an evaluation of where she is in terms of the concrete functions of pricing, money, quantity, and numbers.

Adam: I encouraged her to make out a bill. Lily was ordering some things and Rachel couldn't add up three numbers in a row.

Dr. Otto: Before you go to the adding up of three numbers in a row, consider what you saw in terms of Piaget's conservation. You remember?

Adam: Yes, but it's too advanced.

Dr. Otto: You really have to deal with this on a pretty low level developmentally, and try to help her to understand concepts such as "if you have two liquids and you drop something into one liquid that makes it rise higher, does that mean there is more liquid in one than in the other?" So really start dealing with straight conservation and then gradually bring her up to the point where she will be able to make use of numbers.

Adam: But now she can't really do that.

Dr. Otto: No, and now she's told you she can't. Now you can make use of numbers, start with conservation and then proceed to natural methods of graphing. By that I mean starting to deal with sorting, classifying, and ordering and also graphing. You've got books, or you've got pieces of wood; she can find out how many pieces of wood are one size, she can draw on a piece of paper that same size, and then she can use numbers for that size. What you are doing is developing a graph from the materials you have in your room, you are helping her to understand the concept of the numbers of things, the height of things, and the size. You are again dealing with conservation and you are also dealing with the numbering. You can do the same thing with the measuring of people and graphing that; how many are this big, how many are that size. She's going around measuring children, so here she's going to have another natural kind of grouping.

Adam: We could maybe do a graph of how her plants are
           growing.

Dr. Otto: That's true. I think that's a better idea, it fits in with
           the idea of the project, and that can be extended to
           numbers and so on. You can also develop it, eventu-
           ally, into botany and the labelling of various parts of
           a plant. She can grow a plant on a piece of absorbent
           cotton, then she can see the roots and copula and the
           rest of the plant. These are all things she can deal
           with now.

Adam: Yes.

Dr. Otto: There are some really fascinating things that you
           could do. I saw a beautiful example of seed growing
           and I didn't realize that you could do this sort of
           thing. There is a sponge, a very interesting natural
           sort of sponge, you can buy. I guess it is expensive,
           but you can buy pieces of sponge and then you push
           seeds, big seeds, bean seeds, into the holes of the
           sponge and then just have it sitting in water; of
           course it absorbs the water and the seeds start to
           sprout, and it's beautiful. Another thing that grows
           magnificently is dried corn, in cobs.

Adam: The whole cob?

Dr. Otto: Yes, with the kernels on it. You just put one end of it
           in water and then it starts sprouting.

Adam: Is that right?

Dr. Otto: It's really beautiful. Apart from being a most un-
           usual thing.

Adam: She was asking what kind of seeds she was going to
           grow.

Dr. Otto: Well, she can grow almost any seed. Don't interrupt
           her growing things on her farm because that's impor-
           tant, but you can have extensions of it all over the
           place now, and your classroom can really be a
           growing place — I'm sure that you'll find all the
           children will be interested in it, and then whatever
           plants do grow can be moved from your room to

other parts of the building.

Adam: Yes. Well, this was sort of an evaluation of Rachel, I guess.

Dr. Otto: Yes. She was showing you what she really doesn't know, so you didn't have to test her on an ordinary paper and pencil test. You helped set up a situation which showed you that she didn't know much about numbering, quantity, about the use of numbers, about addition; and likewise she'll also show you how much she does or doesn't know about languages, about reading, about any of the competencies. It's an evaluative technique. It's not saying, "Listen, let's see how dumb you are, prove that you are dumb by not being able to answer these questions," but it really tells the child, "Here is a situation, let's see how it goes," although meanwhile you know what you expect. In other words, you are evaluating this child in terms of your ideas of what a child at a certain age should be able, or could be able, to do.

Adam: I know. I feel I'm bogged down with Lily sometimes. I'm not aware of how she is learning. I only assume that she is using material some way or other.

Dr. Otto: I think one of the things you may be saying is, "Am I going along fast enough? Is she making use of the material I am giving her? What are my goals for this child and how do I know I am reaching these goals?" Well, with her you know some of the things you would expect from her within the next month or two. You have these things in mind. They should be flexible.

Adam: No. With Rachel and all the other children I can see something working, but Lily seems to start out really high and it's difficult to get her off being competent.

Dr. Otto: But she's not competent.

Adam: That's what I mean. To get her to stop —

Dr. Otto: The bravado.

Adam: Yes, you're right.

Dr. Otto: It's as though she should be able to because she says she can; then when she starts to demonstrate what she can do, you can see that she really doesn't understand what she's doing. It's a false impression and it's a way of protecting herself from becoming involved in things that she is either going to fail at or doesn't know or doesn't understand but is afraid to say, "Listen, I don't understand, I need help."

Adam: She's getting better — she does try to use new words.

Dr. Otto: Where do you think she'll go within the next month? From what you've seen now — not the way she represents herself to you, as though she is a totally competent person and can do anything you ask her to do — but now that you know she is not competent and that she is aware that you understand this and haven't rejected her for it, you know more or less the level she's at.

Adam: Yes, I think so.

Dr. Otto: Okay, she's learning words, she's using them.

Adam: I heard a report from another teacher that she came in and tried to use a word. For her to do this, and mix it up and then ask what it means, I think that might be a step for her.

Dr. Otto: It is, because she's not saying, "Listen, I know everything."

Adam: Well, I would expect she would want to understand what she is reading.

Dr. Otto: Asking more questions?

Adam: Yes.

Dr. Otto: What else? Would you expect her to become more involved in other areas?

Adam: Yes. She's doing some cheerleading, and she's involved in a play at school. I don't know if she's been involved before. She also plays with the younger children in the junior room and she enjoyed acting out some things we had done with Rachel and with her. Generally the report has been that Lily seems to be involved with more things.

Dr. Otto: And she has her project with horses, which is branching out into descendants and genetics. She's interested in words and using words, and you can work that into the horse project.

Adam: Yes, she asked "What does descendant mean?" We talked about that, and looked it up.

Dr. Otto: So "descendant" could not only become a language word but could also become a pictorial word in that she could draw the line.

Adam: Draw some pictures of words.

Dr. Otto: Yes, she might also become interested in how the word becomes formed, or how you split words. Something simple, like *can* and *not*. Her project with horses might show drawings of the different kinds of horses. You may want to go to the Museum because they have pictures of ancient horses. They have the whole line developed from a tiny horse right through to modern horses. They have them in three dimensional forms. It's a very fascinating display.

Adam: Yes. One of the things we discussed was about how horses developed, we talked about the breeding, and I could tell that it wasn't something she could really handle.

Dr. Otto: Then you don't go into the breeding.

Adam: She hedged on that and just said, "I would like to draw a picture of a horse."

We talked some more about setting goals: not rigid ones, but exploring an idea of where a child could be after a given length of time. We were trying to develop a realistic "goal" for Amelia, who couldn't seem to draw but showed great imagination when constructing with blocks.

Dr. Otto: What we will try to do is let her think of a drawing, or let her build something and then make a drawing. From her drawing she may be able to cut out a pattern. Then she may be able to copy it onto cardboard, cut out the cardboard and then build. We have separated, we have fractionated, and then we are putting together.

Adam: I was trying to get her to do things like that but I
             wasn't aware of what I was trying to do, which was
             to get her, instead of painting part of the city, to take
             the shapes and cut out pieces of coloured paper and
             paste them on. I've been too hesitant, I think, to do
             things in front of the children. I'm afraid of pushing.
             If I just do it and don't say too much, then they can
             imitate or not. I would just take the shape, trace it,
             cut it out, try it out, and just let it sit there.

Dr. Otto: You could ask her what shape this is, does she like it,
             is that colour a good colour and so on. All those
             kinds of questions, to encourage language, but also
             to encourage imitation.

Adam: I was holding back on these things.

Dr. Otto: Don't. Just recognize the level of the imitation you
             expect.

Adam: And don't worry if it's not imitated.

Dr. Otto: It will be imitated somewhere. In other words, you
             just can't say, "You're at this level, we'll work only at
             that level." No, what you're trying to do is help her,
             and you're going to help her.

Our next session was a long one. Reports on the children and
an attempt to try to straighten out Rachel's concept of "more
than, less than." Lily was now coming to see Adam three times
a week; he was trying to work through ways of integrating her
fear of horses with her desire to be with them.

Adam: I'm going to take Lily and Peter to the Museum.
             Peter wants to see the dinosaurs, and she's going to
             see those horses. She's still a bit uptight about the
             horses at the farm, so I just spoke to her about the
             difficulties we had with the horse, and that I was
             going to try to arrange it so she could just be with
             the one horse and the girl who owned it. They would
             have a nice quiet time, and she wouldn't have to be
             afraid. When I explained that, she was interested, and
             was also interested in the little horses at the Museum.

At first she thought they'd only be skeletons. I said they were models . . . I thought I could take Peter and Lily at the same time.

Dr. Otto: There's a great number of things one could see in that Museum.

Adam: I can't see Peter coming to me more than once a week. He manages pretty well with the one time, really.

Dr. Otto: What does he do the rest of the week now? What is he involved in?

Adam: He likes his swimming and he does go ice skating with the school people. A lot of the children are going twice a week to the YMCA to a special little class where they're doing all kinds of exercises on the mat. I think he likes that. Also, there's the junior room that's nicely set up with large blocks and appropriate toys, and it really looks interesting, he's pretty involved now. We went to the library and got some more books on dinosaurs and Indians. He's quite familiar with the library now — he told me he likes it there. We made a map of Barrie for the Indian trip and I'd like to help him make a map for the Museum trip. Remember me speaking to you about Rachel and discovering that she didn't really know much about numbers, and you suggested using the water and the conservation? I tried that out, and it was very difficult for her.

Dr. Otto: What happened?

Adam: I had beakers of water and asked her if she could fill them up to the same height. She could do that pretty well. I asked her if they had the same amount of water in them. Then I put a cylinder of wood in one of them and raised the level of the water and asked her which one had more water. I felt it was a little like testing — I'm not sure why she found it difficult.

Dr. Otto: What was her answer?

Adam: That the one which was higher contained more.

Dr. Otto: That means you have to go back to an elementary

level, where she will be just playing with concrete things, not trying to make any kind of generalizations or abstractions or formal rule developments or anything like that.

Adam: We talked about her seeds a bit. They did start to grow, by the way, after three weeks, just little shoots. So it's progressing.

Dr. Otto: Lovely, that's great.

Adam: But as far as making a graph of which seeds are going to grow first is concerned, this was too much for her to grasp. I know pretty well what she can do and I know that she can paint blocks and make little farms, so I should encourage her to make more pictures and use more shapes, things like that.

Dr. Otto: Exactly. Give her those kinds of experiences and I think you will find that she will gradually begin to understand how to put things together more meaningfully. Now, with the water experiment, you realize that she is just not emotionally prepared to deal with that kind of abstraction nor has she had experiences built in yet to allow her to cope with such a formal operation.

Adam: I pursued the experiment a little further and asked her if she could measure how much there was in each beaker, using a third beaker — to try to show her that there really was the same amount in each beaker in spite of the wood being in one of them. That was very hard for her and she said, "I'm tired."

Dr. Otto: That would be her way of saying, "I can't deal with it now."

Adam: It's surprising to me that she couldn't understand that principle, at her age.

Dr. Otto: Yes, she looks big enough to realize what you did, and understand the principle involved.

Adam: You know, children four years old can grasp it, or begin to grasp it, and she's nine.

Dr. Otto: And yet she's not a stupid child. She's not a retarded child at all.

Adam: Not at all. She's able to do quite a lot.

Dr. Otto: She's a child of at least average intelligence, but if you hadn't recognized her reaction for what it was, if you had placed her on a specific level because of her age, then she could only have learned by rote, then she couldn't integrate and she'd have had more and more trouble the next year.

Adam: The rote system breaks down, it doesn't give children what they need to understand more complicated things.

Dr. Otto: Yes, and the rote system breaks down when children need to either transfer information or try to generalize information; then they're in a quandary. So you go back to an elementary level, where you begin to show them in a sensory way, a motor way, a touching way, a feeling way, all the things they have missed, where they can pick up things they had never really learned adequately, if they learned them at all.

Adam: Well, Amelia has gone back to that level and it has worked very well with concrete things. She took some blocks and put them together to make a little playground; she did very simple things. She's been doing some building outside of our time together, at home. I've decided to see her twice a week also. She's invited me over to dinner at her house, so she's getting quite a lot from it, really. I have been reassuring her more that she has been doing nice things. She hasn't been asking me so much about changing the time and so on. Oh, by the way, I took Anne to a concert Saturday night.

Dr. Otto: How did that go?

Adam: She enjoyed it quite a lot. She had fantasies of the man up on stage looking at her. It was a wild, ranchy rock concert — they were encouraging a lot of acting out. It was pretty shaky for our children, but she got involved in clapping. I don't think she can do much more, she's so down.

Dr. Otto: But gradually that will change, as long as you give her the freedom, the kind of nonpushing, and yet the ability for her to come with you to such things as a concert. That involves a kind of expectation, which she is going to be able to handle.

Adam: Okay then, about Rachel — I guess once a week is enough for her?

Dr. Otto: Unless maybe you could help her to come back more, otherwise leave it at once a week.

Adam: The seed project is really beyond her. She's barely interested in the fact they're growing. One of the staff has been helping her. He's worried because Rachel's been eating the wheat seeds and he's afraid there won't be any left. So I guess I'll just encourage her to play more.

Dr. Otto: Yes, to play more and paint more, to use constructions, to paste things together, and you can encourage her to put them into her book. The book is really serving as a sort of tying together, a bringing together of things she has accomplished, has been successful with. It's important for her to recognize what she's done.

Adam: She wanted to play restaurant again. I'm wondering what she was getting from that. It seems she just wants to take an order and that's that.

Dr. Otto: Let her take orders; let her print the orders, use numbers. Let her make up menus, look for recipes. Let her write a recipe book. Let her try to cook. Extend it in all these different ways.

Adam: You mean let her put things in her book, then. Because they've been using a blackboard for that kind of work.

Dr. Otto: Well, that's fine. I think they should use the blackboard, but they should continue with the book, too, because that's the string that pulls so many things together and gives children a pathway to help them look at what they've done.

Everybody but Anne was making gains this session.

Adam: Rachel is in really bad shape.

Dr. Otto: What do you mean?

Adam: She's doing a lot of acting out at home and in the school, and everybody's angry with her. I became angry too. Rachel's pretty hard to be with right now. She wanted to play restaurant, something she falls back on when there's nothing else to do. She said, "Can I get somebody else to play with us?" I said okay, and she went and got Jimmy; and of course he didn't know what to do and we couldn't really play properly. I thought we should move on a little. "We'll do some painting," I said. I didn't say it exactly like that, I kept asking her what she'd like to do. It was a time for me to take over and I was uncertain of the relationship, I wasn't sure I could help her in that way, but now I think she could have used direction from me and accepted it. It was a hard time for her, it would have been good for me to have been stronger and to have taken over for her then.

Dr. Otto: To have moved in and created a more structured force.

Adam: I did that eventually, and she worked very nicely for nearly an hour. We turned out quite a few paintings. I became involved with my own painting and she did a lot of mimicking.

Dr. Otto: So what looked like a pretty disastrous situation turned out to be more of a productive one.

Adam: Yes, it was. That's what I'm starting to learn — all the different ways to be.

Dr. Otto: Yes, depending on the needs of the child.

Adam: Sometimes you need to be pretty strong.

Dr. Otto: Yes, at times I think you really have to bring in a structure and at other times you have to make the structure fit the child. I mean if the child is unable to deal with the structure of, say, reading, at that moment, then I think you have to recognize this and say, "Well, what we have to deal with now is painting." So you create a structure for the painting. In the case

of Rachel, you created a particular kind of environment which permitted her to play out — paint out,
almost — some of the aggression she was obviously
feeling, by pushing —

Adam: .... throwing the paper all over the floor. I gathered
up all of the paper and hung it on the line afterwards, because she wasn't able to do any clean-up.
Some of the children, Amelia and Lily, are working
on their projects outside of our time, and finishing
them on their own.

Dr. Otto: That's tremendous! That's really good.

Adam: I think it's quite a big thing.

Dr. Otto: That's a tremendous change in their span of involvement.

Adam: Lily made a huge drawing on a 3 by 4 board, and
painted it blue; and she made a port and started
talking about importing and exporting and manufacturing.

Dr. Otto: Great!

Adam: I don't even know where she got the information. She
probably picked up bits and pieces. I can't say for
sure, but I suspect this project pulled all her experiences together. It was a very beautiful thing she did.
It had a wharf with nine arches. It would have been
impressive in an architect's office. The colours were
lovely, all different shades of blue. She left a lot of
space — now I don't know what this would mean,
but I would think it would mean something important, because children usually try to fill space up, and
there was plenty of space to fill.

Dr. Otto You might want to take photographs of this project.

Adam: I've been planning to do that.

Dr. Otto: Do you have a Polaroid camera?

Adam: No, but I can get one.

Dr. Otto: Take photographs then, and keep them to show the
progress that the child makes.

Adam: Amelia and I have been working down in the basement; it's more comfortable there now, but it's still a

somewhat scary place. We worked on one of the things she wanted to do. People kept asking her what it was and she was angry when they thought it was a town. Anyway, she is becoming interested in sculpture. I've introduced her to the word, and she made a mobile that other day. She likes the shape, she likes the concrete feeling, and she likes to experiment with it. She likes to get parts of the mobile tangled up, but when they become too tangled, she's disappointed. She made the mobile and just directed me to help her. Then she made something that looked like a town, but it wasn't a town to her. It was more than that, it was a sculpture as well. It was on a board and it had a lake in the middle. She saw Lily's project and so she left a lot of space, too.

Dr. Otto: But imitation of peers. That kind of thing you were seeing with the two girls, one imitating the other, only comes about because you have permitted it to happen. You have given them proximity to each other so they can watch what's going on, and then they can start to incorporate things that others are doing. It is not so much a straight "I'm taking from you," but "I added on to, from what I see you're doing," and that kind of learning we think of as being much more important and valuable than where a teacher tries to direct a child. So it's the peer/peer interaction learning that really means something.

Adam talked about some new children he could work with, one of whom showed a definite interest but was hedging. The child wasn't quite ready yet, wasn't prepared to accept help at this point. Adam let the child know that he was available to him. Allan came back, which pleased Adam very much. It looked as though this time they would definitely make a start.

Adam: I haven't done much for Anne. I haven't done much for her at all.
Dr. Otto: Help her at her level. Help her by being available.
Adam: She was feeling pretty unhappy one day, and I of-

fered to make her some tea and —

Dr. Otto: But that's really good. I hear from other people that
there is the need for her to be with you. The need for
her to be involved in something that is going on is
important, and that seems to be having it's own positive effect. Do you know much about Anne's background?

Adam: Very little.

Dr. Otto: She said that she wanted to be a singer once.

Adam: At some point I think it might be interesting for you
to look at her background, because I think she is a
girl who may have music in her background. It may
be that if we try to encourage an interest in music, it
may be encouraging her into repression. It's a very
complex thing, where a child will act out against
somebody by studying music, but at the same time he
or she is following somebody's orders in the studying
of it, or vice versa. It might be interesting to try to
find out if there are other things that she would like
to become involved in. Not in the sense of a project,
because I don't think there is anything, right now,
that we could extend into a project.

Adam: No, not at this point. Peter has made a big change,
he's started to build things: He built what he called a
city. We went down to the basement and he ham-
mered away. He's quite good with a hammer, and he
had some good ideas; he didn't finish his project and
we put it away. So I said, "Well, should we complete
this project, let's say on Monday?" because I thought
he was getting quite involved in it. But he didn't
want to do that anymore. He had brought in a set of
plastic tomato baskets, do you know what they look
like?

Dr. Otto: The ones with the loops or the squares?

Adam: It had squares. He left it there on Thursday, when we
went home, and someone had cut it up. It gave him
the idea to finish cutting it up, and he wanted to
make a car out of it. So we went down and started

working on that. And as he looked around the work-
shop for parts that he wanted, he changed again, and
started doing something else. He's got two other
things that he hasn't completed, but he says that he'd
like to get on with something else. So I just said that
I'd keep them for him.

Dr. Otto: Right.

Adam: Lily has been working on concepts, like space.

Dr. Otto: Really. In what way?

Adam: Well, it's interesting. Remember I talked about her
leaving a lot of space on her project, her waterfront?

Dr. Otto: Yes.

Adam: The space idea — it seems to me like something she
can relate to. It is a hard thing to think about, for a
child to think about.

Dr. Otto: Yes, it's so abstract, to think about the emptiness of
space or the difficulties of having one thing adjacent
to another and having space in the middle.

Adam: There was a book on the shelf that she just picked up
and started working on. What has happened is that
instead of me teaching her, she has started teaching
me. I've been a student, and she has actually given
me a couple of tests that she made up. She had to
figure it all out: first of all she could draw it on the
board and I would copy it; and then she would take
home my writings and things that she had told me to
do, and make a test out of it.

Dr. Otto: But in order to make a test out of it —

Adam: She had to know what to do.

Dr. Otto: Exactly! She has to know how to deal with it. She
has to know how to write, how to understand what
she is asking you.

Adam: Yes, she did a lot of writing and she did a lot of
reading, and she was able to change a rigid situation
to where, if she got stuck, then I would just become
the teacher.

Dr. Otto: Right.

Adam: And that's the way it went. I would just say, "Well,

this is what this means, and this is how to spell that,'' and then she —

Dr. Otto: And then she was able to accept this, and continue as soon as you gave her a bit of information, she was able to follow through on a higher level, to make use of your instruction.

Adam: Yes.

Dr. Otto: Very nice!

Adam: We also talked more about the trip to the planetarium and to the Museum to see the horses.

Dr. Otto: That's fine, and it follows; it is a logical evolution of the projects she has been involved in in terms of space, in terms of openness, in terms of now, the term *space*, in terms of our universe, and her interest in horses. I think you've combined it very well.

Adam: Amelia was having a hard time last week. She wasn't able to get involved and was having trouble settling down to do anything at all. We talked about what kinds of things she'd like to do. I think she could use some more puzzles.

Dr. Otto: You might want to help her make her own puzzles.

Adam: That's a good idea.

Dr. Otto: You know, she can make the drawing on a piece of cardboard or on a piece of paper and then she can cut it out and fit it back together again.

Adam: Which would satisfy her a lot.

Dr. Otto: Yes, you'd get several things going on in terms of visual motor coordination and integration of pieces, in terms of cutting and then taking these fragments and putting them together. You would also be able to help her in terms of language, because you'd be doing a lot of talking when you were doing this; the communication of this is extremely important. Then she can go from the picture puzzles to using other kinds of puzzles. You may want to use this technique with some of the other children — taking whole phrases and sentences they use, like "I am being seen,'' and let them write each word, then glue them onto paper and let them build sentences as a result.

This puzzle game can be carried even further, a kind of scrabble game using simple sentences like "I am here" or "John is going out," so the children don't have to deal with spelling but are involved in syntax. It can be a scientific puzzle, for instance, "Does a test tube belong with a bunsen burner?" It can work into analogies of thinking, logical thought processes and is an excellent complement to a project: if someone is working on a farm project, you can deal with it in terms of farm influence: understanding farm knowledge, farm geography, scientific information on soil conservation and so on.

When Adam and I met again, he and Lily and Peter had just returned from their visit to the Museum.

Adam: We had the whole day together. We had a really nice time. We ate in a special restaurant, and then we went to the planetarium show . . . Oh, and we saw a little film strip about horses. We really outdid it.

Dr. Otto: Your project had gone better then, or further, than you'd planned?

Adam: Yes.

Dr. Otto: Well, that's marvellous!

Adam: We had already talked about the horses being smaller and had seen a picture and knew what they looked like, so it really wasn't all that new to Lily but it made it more concrete, I think, and it was somewhere else besides the school — I'm not sure that that is important.

Dr. Otto: It is, it is! I think it's important that she knows that knowledge is somewhere else than just in that school. Yes, I think that's really very important. Could she talk about it in a meaningful way? Could she relate what you had talked about in the school to what was going on in the Museum?

Adam: Yes, and we started dealing with binomial nomenclature and class terms for genus and species for the horses and zebras. She's done very well. She's very interested. I think since I saw you, we went to the farm again. They had Leslie, the girl who owns the horses, take Cricket out of the corral and put her on a lead for Lily to play with. She just played with the horse for half an hour straight, all by herself, she was really getting interested in riding it and things like that. This summer she'll probably do a lot of riding. She really picks things up and works them out on her own — goes to the library and gets books about them. Peter did something the week before the holiday. He said, "I want you to buy something for me, and just surprise me." He was very direct. I said I'd think about it and try to see what I could get him. I had thought of getting a few things but I had forgotten. And I said, "How about if you and I go and get something together?"

Dr. Otto: But that wasn't the same thing.

Adam: No, that wasn't the same thing. We went and got a kite, but I should still go out and get something.

Dr. Otto: What sort of things does he like? What sort of things is he using right now?

Adam: He made a picture, and then a puzzle out of it. Otherwise, I don't really know what would be significant.

Dr. Otto: Does he show any special interest in long kinds of objects?

Adam: He made the snake before, but hasn't really done too much with it.

Dr. Otto: Then you might want to go to the Museum, to the minishop, and buy him a replica of a snake, I think that they have them; or there are snakes that are on poles, the Chinese ones that move; that sort of thing. I think you might find that would be a gift for him he could understand and would be meaningful for him.

Adam: Well, when we walked into the store he chose a kite.

Dr. Otto: Maybe he's demonstrating his freedom!

Adam: Amelia's moving along, she's quite open to doing anything that we can do together. She's been asking me, for instance, to go for a walk. We had a nice walk down to Woolworths; we bought a ruler and discussed how to pick one, considered how much money she had, and then we went around and priced yardsticks. One hardware store was selling them for a lot of money. But you know, I think Rachel is the hardest one to do something with right now.

Dr. Otto: In what way?

Adam: She's quite anxious and running around. In the house she has been very aggressive: she's been pulling chairs out from under people, or doing some pretty dangerous things to people, and she needs to be watched closely. People are shocked at her. I try not to be shocked at her changes, and try to be accepting. It's harder to be in touch with her, to figure out what's going on with her, to help her do anything. When we get together she seems to be more at a loss than she used to be. I've tried to help her keep this little garden going, but it doesn't work. She is interested in planting some more, and in a different kind of pot, so I guess I can take it from there.

Dr. Otto: Yes, put it into a flower pot.

Adam: We're going to put the regular flower pots together, with different kinds of seeds. I can get her quite a variety. She does enjoy watching them, and keeping track of them, but it doesn't seem as though she can use the whole hour. She used to be able to use that and more.

Dr. Otto: You're finding it more difficult to involve her in more things.

Adam: Yes, she comes in for a minute and then has to go off for awhile. There are things that she can do. I mean she will plant the seeds, but if I suggest other projects there are a lot of "Nos" or "no, I don't want to do that." Once, I think I told you, I just got out the paints and she started painting too. I think that's what I need, to just go and do something myself for her.

Dr. Otto: Be careful with some of the children who are starting to do things by themselves, planning and organizing by themselves, it doesn't mean that all of them will always continue in that way.

Adam: No, Rachel has gone backwards, I'm afraid.

Dr. Otto: We have a tendency to say, "Well, if she's done it before, then why can't she still do it?" So be careful of that because that's what we do as teachers all the time, and it's hard to be aware of it.

Adam: It's harder to appreciate Rachel's growth, even though it's a step back in order to pull something together. I'd just sit in the room and say to myself, "Well, I'll just take it easy and she'll come in and out." Lily's been working on her books; Peter hasn't done anything with his books. It's harder to get him involved in it.

Dr. Otto: I can assure you that the book is important. Whether or not he puts things in it all the time, it's always forming the background for him. So don't assume that it's lost its importance. The way in which it is important changes, but it is still the background.

Adam: People talk about him, you know: "Boy! That's an interesting kid! He's a real genius, he puts this together and that together!"

Dr. Otto: He's got the background, he's got the stability to move the figures on the background, and so more and more things will be recognized by the people who live with him.

Adam: Anne has been really as difficult as she can be. I took her out. I hadn't done anything with her in the school and so I invited her to do something for an afternoon, and we went out and did various things. I was just exhausted after being with her. I don't know how to describe it, she was a — well, everything was pretty unpleasant, but she was really depressed.

Dr. Otto: And so, "Everything has to be pretty miserable and pretty bad, because I am so bad?"

Adam: Right.

Dr. Otto: And does she create situations that are eventually going to rebound at her? For instance, if I tell you you're not worth anything or you can't do anything or you can't help me, that's going to make you feel pretty bad about how you're feeling about me and what you think you're doing for me. So eventually you have to say, "Well, I can't do anything for you, I'm sorry." So there is a movement away from her, and then she says, in a sense, "There isn't anything anybody can do for me. I am just a bad person."

Adam: That's why I decided to go out, because around the school nothing could happen.

Dr. Otto: Her hostility expression is very important.

Adam: She's got to have more energy to work this thing through —

Dr. Otto: But it is going along all right

Adam: Yes, it is.

Adam was experiencing the sense of fragmenting you often get when working with disturbed children: pushing ahead and falling back, acting out and holding in. He made an astute assessment of Peter.

Adam: I think that perhaps Peter might take a few steps backwards over the next couple of weeks. He's been holding himself together pretty well.

Dr. Otto: Why do you think he might do that?

Adam: I think he needs a chance to relax a little bit and go back and integrate some of the gains he's made, because he has really moved pretty quickly and everyone has been a little astounded; but I think he'll still want to get a little younger or go back to doing some things he's missed out on. I think he's missed out on a lot of things.

Adam: I've been thinking — talking with the others on staff — about how some of the children need to be able to wander around the school and have nothing to do. I think that's very hard to get used to.

Dr. Otto: For teachers to get used to?

Adam: I think for everyone. Some of the children really do need a lot of that.

Dr. Otto: What they're really doing is looking at their environment, seeing what's there, feeling it out.

Adam: Peter had a shaky time for awhile. He came in and
sat down and we had a chat for a while, and he
wanted to tell me some riddles. I gave him a riddle
book; he started looking at it and reading it; occasionally he asked me the words. That's the first time
he has sat down and really read. As he finished that, I
handed him the old, very elementary dictionary that
we had worked on in a game kind of way a long time
ago, and he got quite involved in that and started
recognizing that all the "*c*s" were together and all the
"*b*s" were together and wanted to know what some of
the things meant.

Dr. Otto: That's tremendous, really.

Adam: So all his trips to the library and looking at things —

Dr. Otto: Looking around and doing things, and classifying
and sorting — that's what he was doing when he was
looking at your early type dictionary.

Adam: Yes. It was a good session. Now Rachel just hasn't
used me. I've set up times but she always has something else to do. I'm still available, but I realize she's
not doing anything with me at all. It took me a
while, I thought it was just the schedule or something like that, but she really is avoiding me. I can't
do anything about it except ask her and set up sched-
ules. I'm just letting her go on. Actually, I looked at
some of her paintings she'd done in the art room, and
they're really outstanding; I should bring some in.

Dr. Otto: Make a collection of them, if she'll let you.

Adam: There's some really beautiful use of colour and interesting ways of putting things together. So she's doing
things, although she's not using me in that regular
way. She gained something from what we did.

Dr. Otto: Don't underestimate the things that go on, on this
unconscious level, I'll call it.

Adam: In these little chats —

Dr. Otto: You see, it's difficult for most of us, because we want
to see the effects of what we do. When we're working

with children we just have to realize that there is another level and another process, and it needs you, as the teacher, to be consistent in your approach to the child, even though it looks like, on the surface, nothing is happening. However, just below the surface an enormous number of things are happening.

Adam: In the last week Rachel has been going through a tremendous change; she's bringing out a lot of really angry feelings and she's hurting people; we're going to have to watch her very closely, she's really quite dangerous. But she's also doing those lovely paintings.

Dr. Otto: Yes, but that's not really unexpected in terms of what we originally said about Rachel. You remember that she was this nice, sweet, beautiful-looking little girl.

Adam: Who got involved and made all these things, but didn't *really* get involved. At that level, the superficial kind of level, she could manage, but now she's much deeper.

Dr. Otto: Yes, it's a deeper level, a much more involved level, a real level; and it's a level that will make her, or permit her, to become an effective woman. Otherwise you have to say, "Okay, these are the rules of the game, Rachel, you play these rules with society and you'll be okay, in the sense that as long as the society stays that way and you know the rules, you can play the game." Now maybe one could say that, but we don't know or think that that's the way in which children really work or really live, because all the rules are always changing, the demands change, all these things always change, it's in a state of change. So what we're trying to tell her now is not so much "You learn rule 1, 2, 3, and 10." It's much more "To see you, let you be the real person, and let you respond as a real person." In this way you won't have to worry in the sense of "Do I understand?" You will understand, because you'll be responding as an involved person.

Adam: Now who else haven't I talked about with you? Oh
           yes, Anne. I haven't done anything with her at all.
           Just talked about doing things on the weekend, like a
           friend would, but she's never really said yes, strongly
           enough, so I just keep offering my help in a very
           gentle kind of way, without any pressure at all. I
           don't think she wants to do anything. Even to go out
           for a milkshake would be a lot for her to do. So I say,
           "Well, why don't we do something?" and maybe
           she'll say, "Maybe I'd like to go horseback riding?"
           So I say, "Maybe we can do that." Then two minutes
           later she says, "You know, I'm really afraid of
           horses." She doesn't know what to do with herself at
           all — basic functioning, managing to get by.

Dr. Otto: And recognizing the overriding depression.

Adam: Yes, and keeping the relationship going.

Dr. Otto: With the support of your relationship, and with
           others, she will be able to do much more, although it
           will take a little while for her to recognize the sup-
           port of those relationships because her early life has
           been such a chaotic, disrupted, lost life. When a child
           loses a parent, and Anne lost a parent —

Adam: Yes, her mother, when she was quite young.

Dr. Otto: Her father — not only is it difficult to trust, and not
           only is it difficult to extend what she has to try and
           maintain the balance, but how do things continue
           for her? Without the strong support of continuing
           attachment, it is almost like the child is unwilling to
           say, "Well, I'll go along and find out what exists."
           It's more like, "I'm going to stay here and make sure
           I've got here, even though what I've got is difficult
           for me to hold onto, hurtful to me, makes me feel
           lousy. I feel generally depressed, but I'm afraid to go
           on." It's like boxing oneself in. It's a kind of rigidity,
           and that rigidity doesn't permit her to explore. She
           can say, "I'd like to ride horses," but as soon as she
           has said that she immediately becomes frightened,
           because that means she has to go out of her little box.

Even though her box is not safe, it's the safest thing she has. She has lost so much, she is afraid she might lose this little box. The new experience —

Adam: That would be a big risk.

Dr. Otto: That's right. Now if she allowed herself to enjoy things. No, it's almost, in a way, the therapeutic relationship she is going to have to explore, "Maybe I was the cause of the separation." It's a punishing of herself. Now that means she can't go on and learn, because anyone who has to punish herself in that kind of a strange way can't really permit herself to recognize that, "I can learn, I can go on, I can become an effective person." It means "I have to hold back because I don't deserve any kind of enjoyment, I don't deserve any kind of pleasure." Such a person gets involved in what looks like delinquent acts, but are, unfortunately, suicidal acts. Not suicidal in terms of now, I don't mean that she's going to jump off the roof.

Adam: But it's a process of dying, more than a death.

Dr. Otto: Yes, I think that's a very good way of saying it.

Adam: Well, it seems that I do very little with her, again. But it is something that she does have.

Dr. Otto: You are working with her.

Adam: Yes, in some way or other.

Dr. Otto: And you become important, even though it is difficult for her to say you are important, and that importance is extended, you know, in the relationship, and that will extend into learning for her. She isn't a stupid child. She's a fairly bright, adolescent girl.

Adam: Do you know Mike ———? The other day he came up to me and he asked me, "When are we going to get together and do something?" And I said, "Whenever you're ready." And that's happened about three times. The other day he came up and said, "Hey, I'd really like to do something, when are we going to?" in a much different tone. So I've set up a time with him now.

Dr. Otto: That's really great, that you were able to do it that way and let him demonstrate when he was ready. Through all those other times, he was really telling you, "I want you to know I'm thinking about it, but I'm not really ready." When he was prepared, you recognized it.

Adam: We had a talk about the things he wanted to work on, geography and math and so on.

Dr. Otto: You can approach them together.

Adam: I spoke to him about that, I said, "What are some of the other things you are interested in?" And he said he was interested in experiments. So I think I overwhelmed him a little bit; there are a number of experiment books around, and I got them out; and I made a mistake — I should have brought out just one. I've done this before, with Peter. I remember him being interested in snakes and I —

Dr. Otto: ... brought in all the worldly books imaginable about snakes.

Adam: Yes, but he did take a look at them and it seems to me what usually happens in that first interview is that the child says what he thinks I'm going to expect from him. And they never follow through on any of these things. So I don't know what he'll do when we get together.

Dr. Otto: What you might want to do is actually learn, or brush up on if you have to, soil discrimination. I don't think that's the actual term; you get some test tubes and you bring in some batches of soil from around the area. Then you try to see whether they contain iron or sulphur or whatever by dropping the various chemicals in, and you get a certain colour, which means you have this or that soil content. That combines experimentation, geography, mathematics, immediacy, because he'll be writing, and he'll be drawing the number of drops and so on. So when you do it that way, you have immediacy. That's the most important thing in this case; it also has to look scientific. You've got the test tubes and perhaps a little rack that the test tubes fit into. It needs to be eye-catching. In other words, I want to catch this boy. I'm going to do it in as unsubtle a way as I can, so I make it look like a laboratory, his idea of a laboratory. Most children think of it as test tubes, and a flask and beaker and a test tube holder and a rack, and maybe a bunsen burner and so on. Nothing complicated in the sense of a huge chemistry set.

Adam: Yes, that would be science to him.

Dr. Otto: The science combines the subjects and starts where he's interested. I feel it becomes really important to start where the boy is interested. An interest expressed in what he sees and you seeing the intellectual, the emotional, the level of "ready." And that's where your discrimination as the teacher becomes so important.

Adam: I think there's enough apparatus to make an interesting enough thing. He could at least do some weighing of the soil. Different soils for different volumes. . . .

For the purposes of this book this will be our last session, but Adam and I continued on for many months, discussing, probing, exchanging information. At this point in our journey with these children there were some very visible positive gains, a stalemate or two, and another challenge coming up. I chose this moment, this session, because to me, it reflects the reality of life. As I mentioned, though, all of these children came through to evolve healthy, productive lives for themselves.

SECTION III

CHAPTER 9

PARENTS AND EDUCATION

THE obvious value of play-oriented teaching techniques seen in Chapter 8 is a far cry from the disillusionment of child and teacher outlined in Chapter 7. Neither culturally deprived nor culturally satisfied children can learn effectively when the materials they are given are unknown to them. They cannot learn effectively when their very mode of learning — through play — is taken from them and replaced by a system which is more concerned with what they learn than how they learn.

We could stop here and relegate blame, responsibility, and lack of insight to government officials and educators. But, in truth, a system reflects the society it lives with, so eventually we must look at that society itself, the adults in whose hands the children are placed.

The problem of education and educating young children is many pronged. First, adults, parents and teachers alike, have to be helped to understand that play is the essence of learning for children. The purpose for which play serves is manyfold, not only promoting academic learning and concept formation but also social interaction, self-understanding, and acceptance. I have given a detailed description of this in Section I.

Second, we have to try and make educational goals relevant to parents' expectations so that the child will be able to make use of his drive to learn and explore, yet not be made to feel anxious or different from his parents. Too often the child will come home from school talking about some piece of information to which his parents cannot relate at all.

Third, schools and teachers must be made more potentially effective through provision of the space and materials which encourage play and an emotional atmosphere which promotes it. It is the atmosphere, the emotional attitude which encour-

167

ages learning, and parents and families have to be helped to
understand what is meant by this.

Much of the carefully structured and rather rigid curriculum
planning and classroom timetabling devised over past years
needs to be reconsidered and some of it will have to be discarded. It is this rigidity which has prevented many children
from learning. Too often, the children's life and their experiences have not been taken into account. Education must
equal the flow of their life experiences at those times when they
are not at home, when they are not out in the yard or on the
sidewalk. Parents will gradually learn, as well, that if our educational curriculum is to be of service to children, it has to be
flexible and adaptable, and that, since children do not compart-
mentalize their life into twenty minute intervals but rather
think of the day as broken up into three meals usually and plan
for work and play in the morning, afternoon, and evening, so
too our educational classrooms should be planned to enable the
children to see the morning as a flow, not as a series of inter-
rupted periods which is not especially meaningful to them. We
are not doing children a service when we break up their lives
this way. We are not teaching them something useful for
living. Rather, we are "boxing" them in. We are timetabling
them simply because it is convenient to adults. We must alter
our thinking as parents so that we permit and encourage education to be at the service of children.

Perhaps the most important first step is that we will have to
discard our embedded "puritan equation" that learning equals
work equals playlessness, and the total and irrevocable separation of work and play which is the corollary to this equation.
This is a moral concept which streams across all classes in our
society: middle-class parents are no different from working-
class parents in equating school and hard work as the necessary
ladder of success in our economic world. Adults will express
guilt if they play: we all know people who explain their need
to play golf or tennis for reasons of health: "It's good for me."

How patently ludicrous is the idea that we must agonize to
learn now and suffer to triumph later. Think of the look on a
two-year-old's face as he carefully fills containers with water

and empties them into each other, of a four-year-old constructing vast empires of buildings with blocks, of a six-year-old examining a wriggling worm in fascination, of an eight-year-old bouncing a ball as hard as she can to see how high it will go. These are children at play, exploring the world they are part of and learning more than we can begin to catalogue from their constant investigations and questions, learning more than we can begin to teach in all our careful curricula. They are playing, learning, enjoying at the same time. Isn't this what life is really all about? Can't we write a new equation which will allow our children to grow into less restricted adults, who can say, "I play golf because I love being outside, moving freely, looking at the sky and feeling the grass beneath my feet, laughing and doing well at something and getting to know other people better?"

As our first step, then, in educational innovation, let us begin to say that learning equals play and it can be fun.

It will be hard for many to accept the premise that the curriculum can be arrived at through cops and robbers, cowboys and Indians, space pilots and frogmen, play with kitchen tools, building block towers, and drawing and painting pictures.

The most important consideration of educational innovation in general is that it is an exceedingly complex field. On the surface it is the terminology, the jargon, that is confusing, as people keep coining phrases and words to describe what they try, or see tried, often without sufficient definition and thought. Underlying this surface confusion are the innumerable variables involving interpersonal relationships and reactions: children, teachers, parents, administrators, researchers — five distinct groups, each with a distinct interest and traditional role to play in public education. These groups have frequently clashed in an attempt to define what the best education is, each group, with reason, feeling they are in a position to know what should or should not be done. Surrounding them is the massed infantry of "the practical" (school boards, taxpayers, governments) ready to translate what they believe may be desirable theory into what is financially and politically expedient in terms of buildings, salaries, taxes. It is a mixed bag of convolutions.

Parents, the numerically largest group, may not be an integral part of the education policy in terms of planning, but their insistence on certain structures in education makes them a politically powerful group. Often unaware of the research and information educators have been gathering for decades, they have only their own experiences to fall back on and this may lead to the concept of "If it was good enough for me, it's good enough for my kids." I maintain it is not good enough for their children.

Parents as a pressure group can be a positive force or a negative one. To be a positive force, parents need to be involved, not simply informed. To do this, they must be involved in ongoing discussions of such concepts as curriculum, the child's needs, the teaching process, content of lessons, the planning of goals, and the assessment of achievement. It is useless, if not hopeless, for discussion to be carried on when parents are suspicious of what educators are doing or if teachers feel that the parents have no business in their classroom. For instance, when parents and educators are talking about curriculum it is important that these two groups start off with the same ground rules, that they both understand what the word *curriculum* means.

What do I mean by curriculum? I suggest it is all those things which happen to a child while he is in and out of school. The in-school experiences are guided, in that the educator attempts to understand how the child experiences certain situations, why he experiences them his way, where he has acquired his understanding, and when he is prepared to move on to new experiences. Curriculum in the school is the total learning that goes on in the classroom and is concerned with the plans, the strategies for giving information and content, the guidelines to give the strategies; it is the way in which the classroom is equipped, the materials that are available to the teacher and the child, and the way in which the classroom changes with regard to the strategies and the preparedness of the child to accept change. Teaching then becomes an involved, spirally affair with give and take between teacher and child. However, this is not the entire story. There is an "outside" curriculum: There are events and experiences happening outside of the school which must be taken into account, and to do this often involves a conversation between child and teacher, and between teacher and parents. It is with an understanding of the outside curriculum that the inside curriculum can make sense not only to the child but also to the teacher and, hopefully, to the parents.

A discussion of style of curriculum, without an understanding of its aims, is academic. I am not being idealistic when I say that I feel the aim of the curriculum is to prepare the child for a meaningful life within his community, to give him the opportunity to know himself, to explore his ability, to extend his skills, to acquire competencies so that he will feel sufficiently confident to go out and try new things, so that his curiosity and creativity will continue to operate throughout his lifetime. This is a practicality immeasurably more useful than teaching him a vocation. Adaptation to society must remain a flexible concept, and since "society" changes so rapidly, we must help the child adapt to his ever-changing environment without losing his individuality, creativity, or understanding.

I suggest further that the curriculum not just wait for changes to occur, rather it must encourage changes, it must lead to new patterns of understanding and knowledge, it must create the atmosphere for useful research. This means that the educator must acknowledge a need to understand what goes on in society and be prepared to alter his aims. The parents must also be prepared to acknowledge change, and that change brings with it new tools. No longer do we need to think of only wooden tables, now we think of plastic tables, and this means we do not worry about scratches or mess on table tops, this means we adapt to the ever-changing environment.

This may imply that there is less emphasis on facts and more emphasis upon helping the child to acquire and discover information by using classroom resources and resource people. However, the routines of the class, the structure of the day, the limits set by the resource people are vital to the child, for if we remove emphasis on fact teaching and remove routines, then we essentially deprive the child of needed anchor points which he uses to integrate new information. Unfortunately, in the rush to assimilate the new awareness emphasis, too many classes left out both facts and routines and thus proved to parents that fact teaching, the old way of teaching, was imperative, for their child came home confused, anxious, and complaining. The child has a need to know where he is, where he belongs, and he has to have this identified clearly. What I am saying is that the structure must change as the child changes and grows, for we eventually want to see a person who becomes increasingly independent and mature, and increasingly able to select and choose, within a guided classroom, materials with which to acquire information and understanding. The school helps the child grow in his culture, and by accepting his culture allows him to be proud of it and to contribute to it. Materials in the classroom, therefore, reflect his heritage, his culture, his neighbourhood, his parents. We make the inside and outside curriculum work together so that what the child brings with him into the classroom is of real value and what he takes home from the classroom relates to his environment there. The classroom is not a foreign place, it is a place of understanding; and with understanding of himself and his culture he can go on to understand and accept other cultures, other people, other languages.

Parents are the multipurpose human beings of our time. If one tried to follow to the letter the role of parent as dictated by psychologists, sociologists, teachers, and politicians, he would have to be all things to all men — and even more to his children. I am not saying to the parents, "You must be all this," just as I would not say to a child, "You must do this in this way." I ask that they open their minds and recognize and value their children's early childhood experiences and their ways of learning. If I say the teacher and child engage in reciprocal learning, so can parent and child. I acknowledge and agree with the demand that children understand numbers, learn to count, and especially, learn to read.

Dorothy Gardner[17] has said in her book *Education of Young Children*, "We are coming more and more to realize that emotional satisfaction lies at the root of all remedial effort. In dealing with the youngest children we do not, however, always take sufficient account of the fact that intellectual satisfactions are essential if full happiness is to be attempted." I agree with her: I think that children do want to learn, they want to progress. If the educational system gives them a kind of emotional satisfaction without intellectual and academic achievement (which happens when the self-discovery method is taken to extremes), I think we rob the child. On the other hand, it does not seem possible to help a child achieve academically without affording him immense emotional satisfaction at the same time. One follows from the other very naturally; it becomes a springboard for further learning, learning that is investigative and enthusiastic, that will automatically lead children to discover the "howness" of things and is deeply rooted from the "inside."

To achieve this kind of educational system, parents must become involved in the schools so that they understand not what their children are taught but how they are being taught, so that they understand the process as well as the product. The only way to do this is by discussion, observation, dialogue, and interraction between parent and educator.

HOW IS A RABBIT?

If, in the year 2001 or so, your child is sauntering on the moon not far from his geodesic moon dwelling one day, and sees a large purple animal with orange antennae and green whiskers and suction cups for feet bounding through the air wearing a sign that clearly says RABBIT, what will be most valuable to him? The old definition of RABBIT (memorized in his school days) as a soft, furry creature with a pink nose and fluffy tail and big feet who eats carrots and hops gently among the greenery? Or the ability to assess independently the "howness" of this new creature and decide, accordingly, whether to play with it, eat it, or run from it? His ability to cope may well depend on our ability as parents and educators to revise our long-held convictions, prejudices, habits, and fears in time to change the educational system into a more open and exploratory way of learning and growing for all children — and for each of us.

BIBLIOGRAPHY

1. Almy, M.: *The Early Childhood Educator at Work*. New York, McGraw-Hill Book Co, 1975.
2. Bernstein, B. and Henderson, D.: Social class differences in the relevance of language to socialization. *Sociology, 3(1)*:1-20, 1969.
3. Bernstein, B. and Young, D.: Social class differences in conception of the uses of toys. *Sociology, 1(2)*:131-140, 1967.
4. Biber, Barbara: Preschool education. In Ulrich, R. (Ed.): *Education and the Idea of Mankind*. New York, Harcourt Brace Jovanovich, Inc, 1964.
5. Biber, Barbara: Challenges Ahead for Early Childhood Education. National Association for the Education of Young Children, 1969.
6. Biber, Barbara and Shapiro, E.: The education of young children: a developmental-interaction approach. *Teachers College Record, 74(1)*:55-79, 1972.
7. Blackie, John: *Inside the Primary School*. New York, Schocken Books, Inc, 1971.
8. Brainerd, Charlotte and Singer, Sylvia: Communication through the use of materials. *The Journal of the Canadian Association for Young Children, 3*:32-40, 1977.
9. Bruner, John S.: *Toward a Theory of Instruction*. Cambridge, Harvard University Press, 1966.
10. Buck, Pearl S.: *The Joy of Children*. Louisville, Bookworld Communications Corporation, 1974.
11. Caspari, Irene E.: *Troublesome Children in Class*. London, Routledge & Kegan Paul, Ltd, 1976.
12. Dewey, John and Dewey, F.: *Schools of Tomorrow*. New York, EP Dutton & Co, Inc, 1915.
13. Dudek, S. Z.: Creativity in young children — attitude or ability? *Journal of Creative Behavior, 8(4)*:282-292, 1974.
14. Erickson, Eric H.: *Identity and the Life Cycle*. New York, International Universities Press, Inc, 1959.
15. Fader, Daniel: *The Naked Children*. New York, Macmillan Publishing Co, Inc, 1971.
16. Frank, Lawrence K.: Role of play in child development. *Childhood Education, 41*:70-83, 1964.
17. Gardner, Dorothy E. M.: *The Education of Young Children*. London, Methuen and Company Ltd, 1962.
18. Glasser, William: *Schools Without Failure*. New York, Harper & Row

Pubs, Inc, 1969.

19. Guthrie, G. M., Nasangkay, Z., and Guthrie, H. A.: Behaviour, malnutrition and mental development. *Journal of Cross-cultural Psychology*, 7:169-180, 1976.

20. Hartley, R. E., Frank, L. K., and Goldenson, R. M.: *Understanding Children's Play*. New York, Columbia University Press, 1952.

21. Holt, John C.: *How Children Fail*. New York, Dell Publishing Company, Inc, 1965.

22. Isaacs, S.: *The Children We Teach*. London, University of London Press Ltd, 1950.

23. Kellogg, R.: *Analyzing Children's Art*. Palo Alto, Mayfield Publishing Co, 1970.

24. Kennell, J. H., Trause, M. A., and Klaus, M. H.: *Parent-infant Interaction*. Ciba Foundation Symposium 33, Amsterdam, Elsevier Publishing Co, 1975.

25. Klaus, M. H. and Kennell, J. H.: *Maternal-infant Bonding*. Saint Louis, C.V. Mosby Company, 1976.

26. Klein, R. E., Freeman, H. E., and Yarborough, C.: Effect of protein calorie malnutrition on mental development. *Advances in Pediatrics*, *18*:75-91, 1971.

27. Lewis, M.: *Clinical Aspects of Child Development*. Philadelphia, Lea & Febiger, 1971.

28. Lewis, M. and Rosenblum, L. (Eds.): *The Origins of Behavior*. New York, John Wiley & Sons, Inc, 1974.

29. Lowenfeld, V.: *Your Child and His Art*. New York, Macmillan Publishing Co, Inc, 1954.

30. Matthew, S.: Education for the Early Years. Barbara Biber, unpublished M.A. thesis, Toronto, University of Toronto, 1978.

31. Parten, M.: Social play among preschool children. *Journal of Abnormal & Social Psychology*, 27:243-269, 1932.

32. Piaget, Jean: *The Origins of Intelligence in Children*. New York, International Universities Press, Inc, 1953.

33. Piaget, Jean: *Play, Dreams and Imitation in Childhood*. New York, W.W. Norton & Co, Inc, 1962.

34. Pinkus, Joan: A Prospective Study of Relationships Between Prenatal Maternal Parameters and Early Infant Development. Unpublished Ph.D. Thesis, University of Toronto, Toronto, 1977.

35. Postman, Neil: *Teaching as a Subversive Activity*. New York, Dell Publishing Company, Inc, 1969.

36. Rogers, R. S. and Wright, E. N.: The School Achievement of Kindergarten Pupils for Whom English is a Second Language: a Longitudinal Study Using Data from the Study of Achievement. Toronto: Board of Education for the City of Toronto, Research Department (Report No. 80), 1969.

37. Rusk, B., (Ed.): *Alternatives in Education. O.I.S.E. Fifth Anniversary*

Lectures. Toronto, General Publishing Company Ltd, 1971.

38. Sharpe, L. W.: The effects of a creative thinking skills program on intermediate grade educationally handicapped children. *The Journal of Creative Behavior, 10(2)*:138-145, 1976.

39. **Spitz, R. A.: *The First Year of Life.* New York, International Universities Press, Inc, 1965.**

40. Stern, Daniel N.: Mother and infant at play. In Lewis, M. and Rosenblum, M. (Eds.): *The Origins of Behavior.* New York, John Wiley & Sons, Inc, 1974, vol. I.

41. Stern, Daniel N.: The goal and structure of mother-infant play. *Journal of the American Academy of Child Psychiatry, 13*:402-421, 1974a.

42. Tolman, E. C.: Cognitive maps in rats and man. *Psychological Review, 55*:189, 1948.

43. Weininger, Otto: A report of some preliminary research into the etiology and treatment of emotionally disturbed children. Unpublished paper presented at the Ontario Association for Emotionally Disturbed Children, Toronto, 1961.

44. Weininger, Otto: How is a rabbit? An approach to the education of young children. *Involvement, 4(4)*:16-21, 1972.

45. Weininger, Otto: Transplant, transformation or transition: the British pacemakers and the Canadian innovators. *The Educational Courier, 43(4)*:8-17, 1973.

46. Weininger, Otto: The endless quest: the evolution of curiosity in childhood. *Journal of Early Childhood Education, 8(1)*:5-11, 1974.

47. Weininger, Otto: The inner city child — hopelessness must not be a way of life. *Education, 96(2)*:113-123, 1975.

48. Weininger, Otto: It's what you feel about what you do that counts. *The Educational Courier, 46(6)*:22-28, 1976.

49. Weininger, Otto: Language development in the classroom. *Journal of The Canadian Association for Young Children, 2*:27-35, 1976.

50. Weininger, Otto: Play and early childhood education. *The Journal of Early Childhood Education, 10(2)*:27-39, 1977.

51. Weininger, Otto and Muskat, Jack: The Madison Avenue school — a school which means hope. *Orbit, 9(2)*:15-17, 1978.

52. White, R. W.: Motivation reconsidered: the concept of competence. *The Psychological Review, 66*:297-333, 1959.

53. White, Burton: *The First Three Years of Life.* New York, Prentice-Hall, Inc, 1975.

54. **Winnicott, Donald W.: *Collected Papers Through Paediatrics to Psycho-Analysis.* London, Tavistock Publications, 1958.**

INDEX

179